W9-CBT-999

HANDMADE MUSIC FACTORY

FEB 1 0 2012

DEWITT COMMUNITY LIBRARY
SHOPPINGTOWN MALL
3649 ERIE BLVD. EAST
DEWITT, NEW YORK 13214

HANDMADE MUSIC FACTORY

★ THE ULTIMATE GUIDE TO MAKING FOOT-STOMPIN'-GOOD INSTRUMENTS ★

MIKE ORR

DEWITT COMMUNITY LIBRARY

© 2011 by Michael Orr and Fox Chapel Publishing Company, Inc.

Handmade Music Factory is an original work, first published in 2011 by Fox Chapel Publishing Company, Inc. The patterns contained herein are copyrighted by the author. Readers may make copies of these patterns for personal use. The patterns themselves, however, are not to be duplicated for resale or distribution under any circumstances. Any such copying is a violation of copyright law.

Published and distributed in North America by Fox Chapel Publishing Company, Inc., East Petersburg, PA.

ISBN 978-1-56523-559-5

Library of Congress Cataloging-in-Publication Data

Orr, Michael, guitarist
 Handmade music factory / Michael Orr.
    p. cm.
 Includes index.
 ISBN 978-1-56523-559-5 (alk. paper)
 1. Musical instruments--Construction. 2. Guitar--Construction. 3. Washtub bass--Construction. I. Title.
 ML460.O77 2011
 787'.19--dc23
                  2011014757

To learn more about the other great books from Fox Chapel Publishing, or to find a retailer near you,
call toll free 800-457-9112 or visit us at www.FoxChapelPublishing.com.

Acknowledgments

This book is dedicated to my good friend, Paul Scalia, who encouraged me to follow through with this project and many other endeavors along the way that led to the book.

Brewing Co., Gary Bartlett, John Traynor, Harrisburg Midtown Arts Center, Keith Stouffer, Chris Noble, Matthew Sim, William E. Orr, Allen Maltman, Christopher Eldridge, Mike's Music of Harrisburg PA, Shane Bordner, Shane Speal, HEXBELT, Mike Couch, Dann Ottemiller, Brendan McGowan, Neil Kreider, Butchy Sochorow, Toubab Krewe, Monkey Lion Productions, Nathan Boose, Sandy Hollow Arts and Recreation for the Environment, Daniel Wilt, and Luther Dickinson. I could not have done this without all of your help.

Thanks to Shane Speal of *www.CigarBoxNation.com* for contributing awesome sidebars throughout the book (see page 20, 23, 30, 37, 38, 43, 48, 78, 89, 94, 102, 110) as well as the gallery of 100% recycled instruments (10–17).

Thanks to Jen Statler, of Jennifer Statler Photography, for allowing use of the images on pages 5 and 92. *www.jstatlerphotography.photoreflect.com*

Thanks to RJ Gibson and Todd V. Wolfson for allowing use of their Purgatory Hill images on page 101.

Thanks to Silver Pop Pop for use of the image of Hymn For Her on page 111.

Thanks to Tricia Perry for use of the image of Homemade Jamz Blues Band on page 117.

Thanks to Sarah Ann Staub for use of the images of Toubab Krewe on page 45.

Thanks to Adam McCullough, *www.AdamMcCullough.com*, for use of the image of Luther Dickinson on page 91.

Thanks to John Byrne Cooke, *www.cookephoto.com*, for use of the image of Fritz Richmond on page 28.

Thanks to Mark Bush for use of the images of Chris Anderson (page 53) and Jack Pearson (page 70).

Note to Authors: We are always looking for talented authors to write new books
in our area of woodworking, design, and related crafts. Please send a brief letter
describing your idea to Acquisition Editor, 1970 Broad Street, East Petersburg, PA 17520.

Printed in China
First printing: November 2011

Because working with wood and other materials inherently includes the risk of injury and damage, this book cannot guarantee that creating the projects in this book is safe for everyone. For this reason, this book is sold without warranties or guarantees of any kind, expressed or implied, and the publisher and the author disclaim any liability for any injuries, losses, or damages caused in any way by the content of this book or the reader's use of the tools needed to complete the projects presented here. The publisher and the author urge all woodworkers to thoroughly review each project and to understand the use of all tools before beginning any project.

ABOUT THE AUTHOR

PHOTOGRAPHS BY JENNIFER STATLER PHOTOGRAPHY

Mike Orr is a professional flooring installer and owner of Built2Last Guitars. He has designed, built, and sold hundreds of recycled-material instruments. The highlight of his career was when guitar legend Luther Dickinson played one of his guitars in front of a live audience. When he is not in the shop, Mike can usually be found touring the music festival circuit in his VW van on weekends.

PHOTO BY JOHN McELLIGOTT/KM PHOTOGRAPHY.

SHANE SPEAL

Shane Speal is a performing blues/rock songwriter who plays a primitive guitar made from an empty cigar box and a stick. He is also the leader of the modern Cigar Box Guitar Revolution, a growing fan base of cigar box guitar builders and players who congregate at Speal's website, *www.CigarBoxNation.com*. Speal has performed concerts throughout the country and has been featured in many TV, newspaper, and national magazine features. He is also the central figure in Max Shores' documentary on cigar box guitars, *Songs Inside the Box*.

DON TOMÁS
CLÁSICO
NET CONTENTS ONE U. S. GALLON
SPIRITS OF
Gum Turpentine
ACCEPT NO SUBSTITUTES
ORIOLE BRAND®
FROM THE LIVING PINE
HARMFUL OR FATAL IF SWALLOWED
READ CAREFULLY CAUTION ON SIDE PANEL
THE WARNER GRAHAM CO.
BALTIMORE 2, MD.

CONTENTS

FOREWORD

BY BRUCE M. CONFORTH PH. D., BEN L. MINNIFIELD, AND DR. TANYA SCOTT—
ROBERT JOHNSON BLUES FOUNDATION

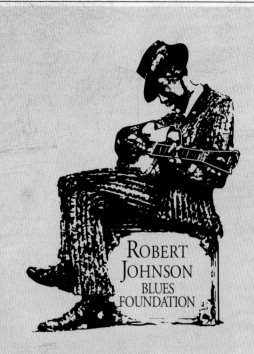

ROBERT
JOHNSON
BLUES
FOUNDATION

As a comprehensive nonprofit organization that protects the legacy and music of legendary blues artist Robert L. Johnson, the foundation also encourages those activities that keep alive the traditions that formed Johnson's music.

This book is about one of those traditions:
HOMEMADE INSTRUMENTS.

The state of Mississippi's mantra is "The Birthplace of America's Music." That credo places the state in a unique arena when highlighting the genres of popular music that have contributed so much to the world of creative entertainment. The instruments that were born out of both creativity and poverty are indicative of the spirit of America and the "can do" mantra that shaped the Industrial Revolution.

2011 is the centennial birthday of this icon force, and this foreword serves as a literary salute to the "King of Delta Blues" and how his ingenuity laid a foundation for greatness.

Blues music has its origin in the work songs sung by slaves in the southern states of America. During slavery, Africans adapted to using the leftovers of plantation owners as mechanisms for survival and entertainment. They also used their own traditions to transform the American cultural landscape. The cultural relationship of slave and slave owner was complex and often a give-and-take exchange. From foodways (using cast-off pig intestines to create the delicacy of chitterlings), to architecture (slaves introduced the "front porch" to America), to folk medicine and traditions, slave culture brought much to American life.

Music was a particularly interesting area of exchange. Although slave owners often encouraged musical expression among their slaves, believing a misguided rationale that a singing slave was a happy slave, they also felt instruments could be used to communicate secret messages that would lead to rebellion. The 1739 South Carolina slave codes, for instance, were the first to ban drumming among slaves for fear that the rhythms would foment insurrection. However, the African musical tradition slaves brought to the New World included much more than just drums. There was a rich African tradition of stringed instruments, from the one-string fiddle to the

"If the blues tell stories about life experiences revolving around race, love, and social class, then these instruments provide the background upon which those stories were sung."

multi-stringed kora. Perhaps the most important of these African retentions was the banjar, which would morph into the banjo—oddly enough, an instrument that would become associated with Anglo-American folk music and ultimately one of the signature sounds of the proto-typical white roots music "bluegrass."

After slavery, though still under the oppression of Jim Crow and segregation, the power of song and music provided a base for inspiration and entertainment. America's earliest documentation of songs from this era is found in Allen, Ware, and Garrison's 1867 book, *Slave Songs of the United States.* In this seminal text, we see work and secular songs, as well as the spiritual roots that would eventually form the blues. This early documentation speaks to music used to open the core of a person's soul through verse and instrumentation, and explore the pain and pleasure of living. This is the basis of the blues.

From L to R *Standing: Steven Johnson, grandson of Robert Johnson & VP; Michael Johnson, grandson of Robert Johnson & Treasurer. Seated: Ben L. Minnifield, VP Global Marketing & Media; Dr. Tanya Scott, VP Global Business Development; Claud Johnson, son of Robert Johnson & founder; Vasti Jackson, Artist & Musical Director. Painting by artist Earl Klatzel.*

It is no accident that at the same time African Americans were creating the lyrical and musical roots for the blues, they were also creating their own ad hoc musical instruments. The earliest extant examples of cigar box guitars, for example, stem from this period (although reported history dates them to just before the Civil War). By the 1880s, plans to build simple cigar box banjoes were appearing in print. While there were, of course, white children who also built their own homemade instruments, the particular poverty of the southern Black made such creations more of a necessity than a social curiosity. If you were a young southern Black growing up on a plantation, and you wanted to learn to play guitar, it was almost a given that you'd have to make one yourself. And this is precisely what Robert Johnson, and so many before and after him, did.

Johnson's childhood friends recall how he took three strings of baling wire and nailed them to the side of the sharecropping shack he shared with his mother, Julia, and stepfather, Dusty Willis, in Commerce, Mississippi. Johnson slid two bottles under the wires to increase the tension, and then picked out tunes on his homemade diddley bow. And while those same friends said they couldn't make any sense out of what he was playing, no doubt to the young Robert it was pure music. It wasn't long after that that Robert got his first guitar, but the roots of his music had been laid on the homemade diddley bow.

The great slide-guitar evangelist Blind Willie Johnson began on a one-string cigar box guitar. Big Bill Broonzy,

Muddy Waters, B.B. King, and so many others did likewise. It's not stretching the point too far to wonder whether the blues would have developed as they did had it not been for these homemade instruments. Mike Orr does a wonderful job of relating this tradition to a new generation of America, updating some plans to include electric pickups, while still remaining true to the underlying impulses that gave birth to the instruments and the music played on them. This book deftly takes us through the creation of these instruments so we can find our own connection with these musical roots.

If the blues tell stories about life experiences revolving around race, love, and social class, then these instruments provide the background upon which those stories were sung.

Robert Johnson's musical acumen came as a result of creating his own instrument to simulate the sound of a guitar. It was that zeal to find solace in music that comforted his soul as he lived a very transient lifestyle in rural Mississippi. It is that same zeal that can be shared through this book.

Bruce Conforth

Ben L. Mifield

Tanya Scott

ABOUT THIS BOOK

Anyone can make a musical instrument and play it—all it takes is some basic instruction (which you're holding in your hands), some inspiration (I think you've already got that, or you wouldn't be here!), some simple tools (you've probably got 'em already), and materials (you can find these at yard sales, swap meets, and even in the garbage). This book specializes primarily in stringed instruments, but there are some percussion pieces as well—in fact, there's everything you need in these pages to create enough instruments for an entire band!

I'd suggest starting out with the simpler accompaniment instruments—the One-String Washtub Bass (page 20) and

Soup Can Diddley Bow (page 30) are quick and easy to build, and don't require many materials at all. The chapter on stomp and scrub percussion (page 38) will show you how to make an electrified washboard and stompbox. After you've got those down, venture into guitar territory—use a cigar box or cookie tin to create an easy-build slide version (page 48, 66). Then, when you're comfortable with all the ins and outs of guitar building, take a crack at creating a more complex fretted guitar (page 78) or lap steel guitar (page 94). Be sure to visit the chapter on Electrifying Your Instruments (page 106) for detailed instructions on adding electricity to the

10

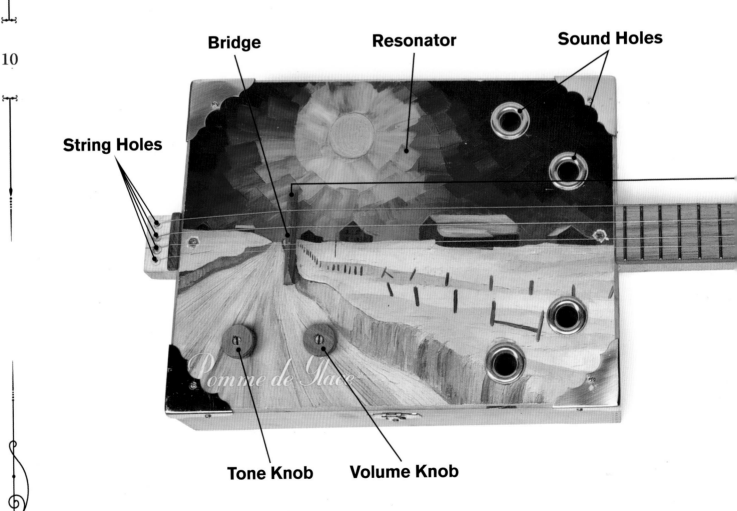

Bridge **Resonator** **Sound Holes**

String Holes

Tone Knob **Volume Knob**

projects—and don't forget to make your own amp by upcycling an old tape deck (page 112).

Along the way, you'll discover lots of interesting music tidbits, scattered on the bottoms of the pages and throughout as sidebars. Keep your eye out for photos of professional musicians jamming on their own handmade instruments, info about other simple instruments you can cobble together, and who knows what else? The King of the Cigar Box Guitar, Shane Speal, chips in periodically with fascinating historical information and other rubber-meets-the-road experiences with the instruments. Don't forget to flip through the amazing galleries of handmade music instruments near the front (page 10) and the back (page 118)—there's plenty of inspiration to get you going! Before you dive in, take a moment to familiarize yourself with the Anatomy of a Guitar, below—it'll help you keep your bearings when you get into the thick of building. Let's get started—and remember, there are no rules! Build it 'til you like it.

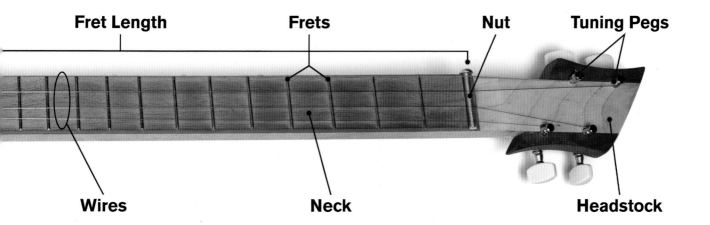

Fret Length   **Frets**   **Nut**   **Tuning Pegs**

Wires   **Neck**   **Headstock**

INTRODUCTION

You may not have realized it, but there is a revolution unfolding right now in the world of music. For many years, it seemed that music was a thing to be purchased—a thing that came in shiny packages, ensconced in CD sleeves and mass-produced guitar cases. Music was something other people did, or something you created on instruments strangers made. The revolution happening right now is taking music off its pedestal and making it accessible to everyone and anyone who is willing to spend a little time with their hands, simple tools, and approachable materials. No longer must you go out to a store to buy your music makers—you can create them right in your own home. This innovative movement grows in numbers every day, as people across the world—hobbyists and professional musicians alike—reconsider their conceptions about music and embark into the world of handmade instruments. Amazing work is happening, as you'll see when you flip through the following pages—each instrument you'll see in this introduction was created for the MacGyver building contest on *cigarboxnation.com*, where the sole rule was that only 100% recycled materials could be used. Handmade music builders are creative and ingenious.

They know that just because standard factory-made guitars have six strings doesn't mean their guitar can't have three, or four, or seven. Instruments can be crafted from old cigar boxes, cookie tins, bedpans, and whatever else you can think of. While today's subversive music makers are blazing a new trail forward, they're also hearkening back to their roots. Before it was common for the average person to be able to afford a manufactured guitar, musicians built their own creations, scraping together whatever they could find to squeeze a note out of. Many famous blues musicians got their starts stretching a screen door wire between two nails hammered into the side of a barn, or on a guitar fashioned from a cigar box and a broomstick handle. So, as you wade into this world of handmade music, remember that all you need is your imagination and whatever scraps you can find—there's no place here for expensive lutherie tools and hi-tech tuning equipment. Don't be afraid to upcycle, recycle, customize, and deconstruct. The sounds you'll tease out of these instruments will be rough, and strange, and beautiful—but one thing's for certain—they will be sounds YOU made.

PAPIER MACHE GUITAR
BY DUSTIN BROWN OF CHICAGO, ILLINOIS

This is a 15" (380mm) concert-scale paper ukulele. The back and sides were cut from black mat board left over from a photo framing project, and covered with veneers made from an old Taylor guitar catalog to give the illusion of Macassar ebony on the sides and maple on the back. The top was cut from spruce left over from a mandolin rebuild, and was finished with expired shellac and stain. The neck was made from black and white mat board laminated together and stiffened with a jatoba floorboard scrap. The fretboard was also cut from jatoba floorboard scrap and fretted with vintage brass frets pulled from an old Kraftsman archtop. A piece of Koa scrap was added to the headplate for a touch of island mojo. The tuners and bushings were reclaimed from an old Yamaha acoustic.

CHICK FEEDER FIDDLE

BY LEE CONNAH OF BALTIMORE, MARYLAND

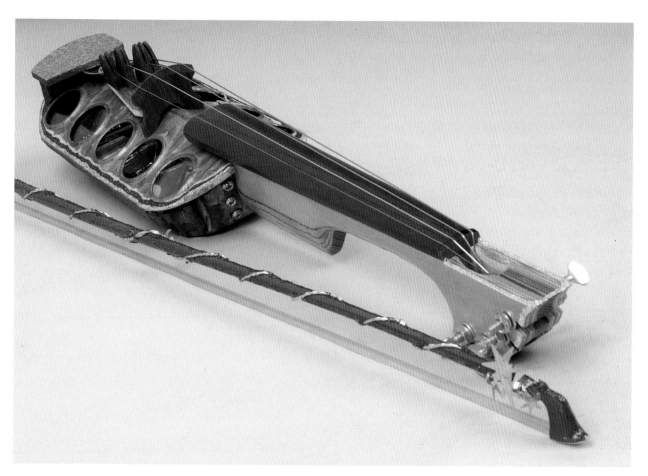

The body is a vintage galvanized chick feeder that was found in an abandoned hardware store. The neck is crafted from scrap plywood and heart pine, with a fingerboard of rejected jatoba flooring—as is the bridge. A spoon serves as the tail piece; stock thumbscrews for tuners; and cork flooring for the chin rest. Miscellaneous scrap wood was used for fine tuners and support. The bow was $5 from a used-instrument store. The decorations include craft store paints, glitter glues, and Mardi Gras beads and mirror shards inside the body.

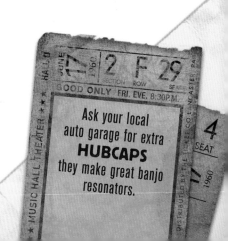

HALL 2 F 29
JUNE 17 1960
SECTION ROW SEAT
GOOD ONLY FRI. EVE. 8:30 P.M.

Ask your local auto garage for extra **HUBCAPS** they make great banjo resonators.

4 SEAT

17 1960

★ MUSIC HALL THEATER ★★★

DISTRIBUTED BY THE TICKET CO. LANCASTER PA.

JUNKYARD DOG
BY WADE COSTENBADER OF CATASAUQUA, PENNSYLVANIA

14

Most parts for this six-string guitar could be found out in the garage. An antique license plate serves as a resonator, with a wrench and bolt for the bridge and nut. A shotgun shell is used to adjust the volume from the piezo contact pickup, which itself was taken from a broken videogame drum set. The neck is fashioned from two broken dowels, saved from being thrown out on garbage night. A hinge and bent nail hold the strings down on one end, while zither tuners from someone else's craft project serve as the tuning mechanism.

One Man's Trash: A History of the Cigar Box Guitar is the **FIRST WRITTEN HISTORY** of the instrument.

BARN WOOD "CIGAR BOX" GUITAR
BY BRIAN WALAK OF PITTSFIELD, MASSACHUSETTS

The resonator is a handmade box, built from an early 1900s barn board. The frets, nuts, and tuning pegs were all old nails purchased at yard sales. Each fret nail was placed in a unique hand-carved groove, since each nail was a different size and shape. Brian noted that the only downside is that the strings tend to break since the tuning peg nails have rather sharp edges—but this would be the guitar for you if you frequently play in bars and get into bar fights!

CANJO
BY NINE-YEAR OLD ETHAN WALAK AND HIS FATHER, BRIAN, OF PITTSFIELD, MASSACHUSETTS

Ethan made his instrument from items his father was throwing away. He cleaned out a quart-size paint can and used it for the body. He found a board for the neck in the scrap bin and some old rope in the garage, which he split for the strings. Nuts and bolts were used to string the canjo.

BACKGAMMON UKULELE
BY RAINER SCHMIDT OF GERMANY

The backgammon game came from a thrift store; the neck was crafted from old mahogany furniture with a rosewood fretboard. A rope is used to keep the game tied shut while being used for musical functions—but as soon as the music is over, the ukulele is easily converted into a backgammon game.

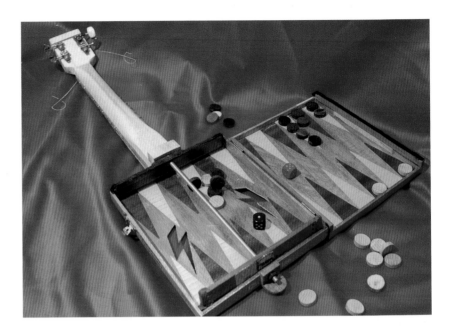

AMMO BOX GUITAR
BY KEN GAFFNEY OF DUBLIN, IRELAND

16

For the resonator, Ken used an old ammo box that he'd kept modeling tools and paints in as a kid. Add some recycled guitar parts and a handful of screws and bolts, and you've got a functional guitar. Ken says it sounds great, and the best feature by far is the storage space inside—plenty of room for a few cans of your favorite beverage.

"SILVER GIRL" UPRIGHT ELECTRIC BASS

BY LEE CONNAH OF BALTIMORE, MARYLAND

Materials used include scrap handrail stock for the neck, four pieces of scrap plywood laminated to form the body, and a found coat rack section for the base. Scrap #10 gauge copper wire was used for the frets and attached with drywall screws. Bicycle quick releases were utilized for the tuners, and dice on an inclined plane for fine tuners. The fret markers are dominoes; the volume control knob is from an old, junked, reel-to-reel tape recorder. Craft store paints and glitter glue, a found metal grate, and a truck stop Silver Girl finish off the instrument.

17

CIGAR BOX GUITAR FESTIVALS are held throughout the US to celebrate the instrument.

ACCOMPANIMENTS

ONE~STRING WASHTUB BASS

The washtub bass is an instrument rich in history as well as sound. It won't take you long to whip up one of these deep-noted beauties, and you'll be glad you did—there's nothing better to accompany a cigar box guitar.

HISTORY OF THE WASHTUB BASS

The washtub bass is an instrument with deep roots in American music, providing the thumping rhythm notes to the early New Orleans 'spasm bands' and the jug bands that came out of Memphis and Louisville in the early part of the 20th century. It later became a central piece in the folk music boom of the 1960s with bands such as Mother McCree's Uptown Jug Champions (which later became The Grateful Dead) and Jim Kweskin & The Jug Band, featuring Fritz Richmond on bass.

The late Fritz Richmond (see page 28) attained status as a true virtuoso bassist. He played with Kweskin, and, later in life, with John Sebastian & the J-Band. Richmond played the instrument with such ferocity that he would go through one galvanized washtub a year! (He eventually remedied the situation by having a washtub factory build him one from stainless steel.) To hear the washtub bass in its full glory, check out John Sebastian & the J-Band's albums "Chasin' Gus' Ghost" and "I Want My Roots."

The washtub bass is again experiencing a resurgence with the popularity of modern Americana music and as an accompaniment in the growing cigar box guitar movement.

MATERIALS

→ Galvanized washtub
→ Wood for the neck, 5' x ¾" x 1½" (1525 x 20 x 40mm)
→ 1½" (40mm)-wide hinge and accompanying screws
→ Nuts and bolts to fit your hinge, 3 sets
→ Extension spring (such as for a screen door), ⅝" x 8½" (16 x 215mm), .080, or bungee cord
→ Nylon clothesline or parachute cord, ⅛" (3mm) braided nylon, 6' (1830mm) long
→ Two large eye bolts with two nuts and two large washers
→ Wood for the legs, three pieces, 4" x 1½" x ½" (100 x 40 x 13mm)
→ Bolts and screws for the legs, 6 sets

TOOLS

→ Tape measure
→ Power drill and assorted drill bits, including ³⁄₁₆" (5mm)
→ Assorted sandpaper, sanding block
→ Pliers
→ Hand saw
→ Pencil
→ Phillips and flat head screwdrivers
→ Adjustable wrench
→ Utility knife
→ Clamp

20

Another name for
the washtub bass is
A GUTBUCKET.

22

PREPARING THE TUB

1 **Remove the handles.** When you have chosen your tub, remove the handles using a pair of pliers.

A HANDY SOLUTION

A washtub bassist once told me that he would buy leather driving gloves and soak the right one in water for an hour. He would then put it on his hand when he went to sleep. The glove would shrink to his hand and provide the perfect plucking glove for washtub bass performance the next day, saving his hand from rope burns!

2 **Mark the bottom center of the tub.** Locate and mark the center of the tub. Use a measuring tape if necessary, but it should be easy enough to eyeball.

3 **Drill the center hole.** Drill an appropriately sized hole for one of the big eye bolts. The hole should be big enough to allow the bolt through, but not much larger.

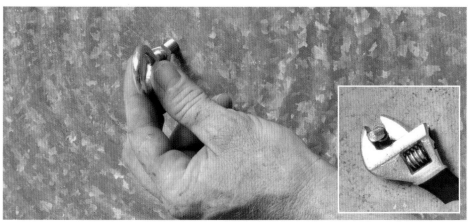

MIKE'S TIP:
Use large fender washers to reinforce the hole for the eye bolt.

4 **Install the eye bolt.** Insert the eye bolt through the bottom of the tub. Slip a washer and nut on the stem of the bolt. Use an adjustable wrench to hold the nut as you tighten the bolt down.

IN AUSTRALIA, the washtub bass is called the **BUSH BASS.**

PREPARING AND ATTACHING THE LEGS

5 **Mark up the legs.** Using the washtub bass leg pattern from page 154, mark two holes in each of the legs.

6 **Drill the holes in the legs.** Using a clamp and an appropriately sized drill bit, drill the holes as shown. Make sure to drill the legs over a piece of scrap wood to prevent splinter-out. If you want, you could also drill each leg separately.

MIKE'S TIP:

An alternate way to attach the legs is to drill pilot holes through the tub and use wood screws to attach the legs.

24

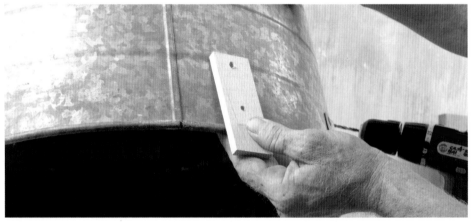

7 **Mark the leg locations.** Pick three equally spaced points around the rim of the tub to place the legs. Line up each leg so there is about 1" (25mm) sticking down below the rim. Mark the two holes.

8 **Drill the leg holes.** Hold the washtub firmly and drill all six holes.

9 **Attach the legs.** Line up the legs with the holes on the inside of the washtub. Insert a bolt through each hole. Install a washer and nut on the outside part of each bolt. Use an adjustable wrench to tighten down the nuts.

PREPARING AND ATTACHING THE NECK

10 **Mark the hinge location.** Line up the hinge so the barrel is on the edge of the neck's bottom.

11 **Attach the hinge to the neck.** If necessary, saw the neck to the proper dimensions. Sand off any splinters. Drill pilot holes for the hinge screws. Attach the hinge with the included screws.

12 **Position the neck on the tub.** Place the neck directly above one of the legs (any leg) as shown. Use a pencil to mark the holes on the bottom half of the hinge.

13 **Drill the tub hinge holes.** Hold the tub securely against one foot to keep it from rolling, or place it feet down on a work surface. Drill the screw holes through the tub.

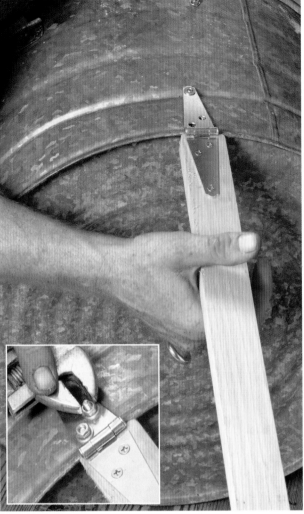

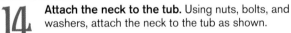

15 **Attach the spring's bottom point.** To install your screen-door spring, attach one end of the spring to the lower bolt on the bottom hinge with a nut and washer.

14 **Attach the neck to the tub.** Using nuts, bolts, and washers, attach the neck to the tub as shown.

16 **Drill the spring's top point.** Pre-drill the hole for the eye screw 3" (75mm) above the spring's top point when lined up with the neck. Screw in the eye screw.

26

The European alternative to the washtub bass uses **A TEA CHEST RESONATOR.**

ATTACHING THE CORD

17 **Attach the spring to the eye screw.** Stretch the spring and hook it onto the eye of the screw.

18 **Pinch the spring eye closed.** Use pliers to pinch the end of the spring closed.

19 **Drill the cord hole.** Mark and drill a hole about 2" (50mm) from the top of the neck for the cord. The hole should be big enough to let the cord through.

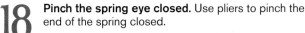

MUSICAL STICKS

If you have any spare thick dowel rods or thick branches lying around, you have the makings of a musical percussive instrument! The most common way to play is to hit a couple of sticks against each other. However, you can even get into pitches by thinning parts of the sticks, or by drilling holes through them. Experiment and see what you can create!

20 Attach the cord. Tie one end of the cord to the eye bolt in the center of the tub. Feed the other end through the hole in the neck and tie a knot.

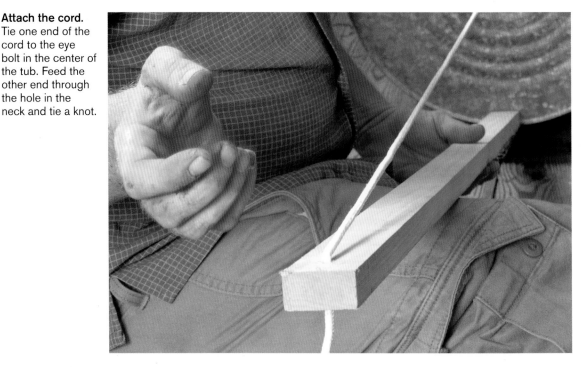

28

★ ★

FRITZ RICHMOND

Fritz Richmond (1939–2005) was king of the washtub bass. He built his first washtub bass in the late 1950s, using a tub, broomstick, and rope. In the sixties, Fritz played washtub bass for Eric Von Schmidt, Geoff Muldaur, Tom Rush, The Charles River Valley Boys, and others. He was a founding member of Jim Kweskin & The Jug Band; after learning to play the jug, he gained nationwide attention by appearing on *The Tonight Show with Johnny Carson* and other national television shows. He went on to perform with The Doors, Bonnie Raitt, Bob Dylan, The Grateful Dead, and many others. He also appeared on Garrison Keillor's *A Prairie Home Companion*. The Smithsonian has one of his washtub basses in its collection.

PHOTO © JOHN BYRNE COOKE, WWW.COOKEPHOTO.COM

HOW TO PLAY THE WASHTUB BASS

To play, stand with one foot behind the tub. Place the other foot on the rim of the tub, toward the front, over one of the legs. Putting your foot here is necessary to hold down the front of the tub while you're putting tension on the center with the string. You could also sit down and hold the tub with your feet on the rim. Hold the top of the neck with your back hand, and use your front hand to pluck the string. To get different notes, adjust the pressure on the neck—putting more or less tension on the string will change the pitch.

If you're concerned about your volume, be sure that your foot is resting on the top rim of the tub only. If you're playing with acoustic guitars only, and using a riser, with no microphone, you can be heard just fine for about 10 yards. The washtub bass will sound very different on a carpeted floor than on a hard one. Some players carry a bass base with them. This is an approximately 36" x 36" (915 x 915mm) piece of plywood covered with carpet, or not, depending on the sound you want. A scrap piece of carpet the same size will also sound pretty good on a wood floor. I suggest experimenting to find the sound that fits you.

29

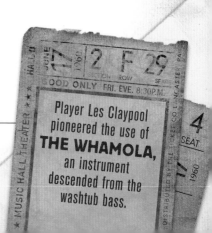

Player Les Claypool pioneered the use of **THE WHAMOLA,** an instrument descended from the washtub bass.

CHAPTER 2

SOUP CAN DIDDLEY BOW

This quick-to-make instrument may seem too simple to be very musical, but it'll fool ya! You can create a lot of music out of one string and some creativity. You'll be experimenting in no time—from start to finish, this baby only takes about half an hour. Grab a can out of the recycle bin, dig out a plank from under your workbench, and get going!

HISTORY OF THE DIDDLEY BOW

In the early 1900s, the poor children of the American South had ways of making music, even when they couldn't afford instruments. The one-string diddley bow was the most basic of these instruments and they made them by nailing a section of broom wire (the wire that holds the bristles to the broomstick) to the side of a barn. They'd raise the string up with bricks or pieces of wood (acting as bridges) and would use a bottle as a slide.

The diddley bow has made appearances in blues history, appearing on several rare and amazing recordings. In the mid-1950s, "One-String Sam" Wilson walked into Joe's Record Shop on Hastings Street in Detroit and recorded two songs, "I Need A Hundred Dollars" and "My Baby Ooh." The recordings featured One-String Sam playing a diddley bow made from a discarded piece of wood and a single string. Sam was later rediscovered in the Detroit slums and invited to perform at the 1973 Ann Arbor Blues Festival. Another lost hero from the 1950s is Willie Joe and the instrument he called The Unitar. Willie Joe recorded several sides using his massive six-foot (1830mm) electrified Unitar diddley bow, most notably on the song "Cherokee Dance" by Bob Landers. In the early 1960s, Eddie "One-String" Jones was recorded on the streets of Los Angeles' Skid Row. Jones' instrument was made with a 2x4, broom wire, and a paint bucket as a resonator. His recordings were later released on the album *One-String Blues* on Gazelle Records. Recently, American bluesman-turned-European superstar Seasick Steve has performed and recorded with electric diddley bows.

Out of all the diddley bow players in history, probably none has mastered the instrument like David "One-String Willie" Williams. Williams is a molecular scientist from Philadelphia and a bluesman specializing in the one-string diddley bow. He has built and performed with replicas of the diddley bows played by Eddie "One-String" Jones, Willie Joe, and several others, sometimes using two bottle slides at the same time! His repertoire includes everything from blues to Bach. See page 37.

MATERIALS

→ Can
→ Piece of wood for the neck, ¾" x 1½" x 30" (20 x 40 x 760mm)
→ Guitar E string (any will work)
→ ½" (13mm)-long flat head wood screws, 2
→ Guitar tuning peg
→ Threaded bolt or skeleton key

TOOLS

→ Measuring tape
→ Power drill and assorted bits
→ Phillips and flat head screwdrivers
→ Pencil

30

5¢ Shine

THE BERIMBAU, a Brazilian monochord vital in Capoeria, is a long bow with a gourd, played with a stone and stick.

MUSIC HALL THEATER ★ ★ ★

HALL B   JUNE 17 '60   2 F 29

SECTION   ROW   SEAT

GOOD ONLY FRI. EVE. 8:30 P.M.

DISTRIBUTED BY THE TICKET CO., LANCASTER, PA.

17 '60   4   SEAT

32

PREPARING AND ATTACHING THE CAN TO THE NECK

1 **Mark holes to be drilled.** Mark two holes; one right above the closed end of the can, and the second about halfway up the can in a straight line from the first.

2 **Drill holes through the can.** Use a power drill to drill the two holes you just marked. The holes should be big enough to allow the threaded bit of the screws through, but small enough so the head can't pass. Drill two more holes on the other side of the can, directly across from the first two, sized to accommodate the shaft of your particular screwdriver.

MIKE'S TIP

Though you can hold the can in your hand and drill, as I did, if you feel uncomfortable with this or if you don't have much practice drilling, there's a safer way: Clamp a sturdy piece of scrap wood about as thick as the inside of your can into the bench clamp. Slide the can over the wood, and now you have a safe and secure way to drill that keeps your hand out of the way.

33

3 **Attach the can to the neck.** Position the can so the small holes are against the wood and the hole in the middle of the can is 1" (25mm) from the end of the wood. The can's open end should be projecting over the edge of the wood. Use a screwdriver to insert screws through the smaller holes into the wooden neck.

THE DAN BAU
is a Vietnamese
monochord with a gourd
and flexible stem used
to change pitch.

BLOWING ON BOTTLES

Grab any bottle, put your lower lip against the rim, and blow across the opening. Similar to singing glasses, you can fill bottles with different amounts of water and change the pitch. If you really like the sound, you can figure out how to strap and connect a bunch of bottles together to make a full set of bottles, similar to a panflute.

34

4 **Mark the string hole.** Make a mark in the center of the can, about 1" (25mm) off the neck.

5 **Drill the string hole.** Place the can securely on a flat surface. Chuck a skinny drill bit in your power drill and drill the hole.

THE EKTARA is an Indian monochord with a split bamboo neck—squeezing the neck changes the pitch.

ATTACHING THE TUNING PEG TO THE NECK

6 **Mark the tuning peg location.** Position the tuning peg on the other end of the same side of the neck, as shown. Make a small mark both under and to the side of the actual peg and then locate their intersection with straight lines. Mark this point. The peg should be about 27" (685mm) from the end of the can.

MIKE'S TIP

Make sure to position the peg far enough off the end of the neck so you'll be able to twist the tuning peg properly.

Place a scrap piece of wood under the headstock before drilling the hole. This will keep the wood from splintering when the bit comes through the bottom of the neck.

7 **Drill the tuning peg hole.** Drill out the hole, making sure to use a drill bit that will give the peg a bit of wiggle room.

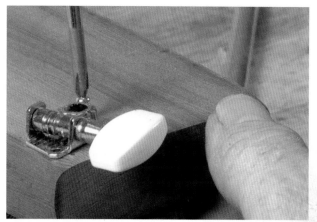

8 **Mark and drill the peg pilot holes.** Flip over the diddley bow so you can see the back of the neck. Mark and drill the pilot holes for the tuning peg's screws. Make sure to use a drill bit just a little smaller than the screws.

9 **Attach the tuning peg.** Use a small screwdriver to attach the tuning peg.

STRINGING THE DIDDLEY BOW

10 **Begin attaching the string.** Feed the string through the hole in the top of the can so the knob on the end of the wire is inside the can.

MIKE'S TIP

After the nut is installed, use a guitar scale template or a guitar tuner to mark the notes on the neck.

36

11 **Complete attachment of the string.** Stretch the string to the tuning peg post and wrap around it three times. Thread the string through the post's hole and pull it tight. Turn the knob to make the string tight. About 1" (25mm) from the peg, insert what a guitarist would refer to as the nut. I used a skeleton key, but you could use a threaded rod or screw. The goal is to lift the string so it can vibrate without hitting the neck.

Use a test tube, pipe, or whatever you wish to slide along the wire.

PLAYING THE DIDDLEY BOW

There are several typical ways to play a diddley bow. Sometimes they are played on your lap like a lap steel guitar, using fingers or a pick and a slide. The legendary "One-String" Eddie Jones played his one-string guitar using a wooden stick to strike the string and a half-pint bottle for a slide. I prefer to tie on a strap and play it like a rock star.

SOME THOUGHTS ON THE DIDDLEY BOW FROM ONE-STRING WILLIE

David Williams, aka One-String Willie, has been playing guitar since 1964 and diddley bow since 2007. He travels to music festivals and has introduced countless people to the sound of the diddley bow. He has written how-to articles about the instrument for several magazines.

One thing to keep in mind when teaching yourself to play the diddley bow (or any other home-made instrument) is Rule Number 1: THERE ARE NO RULES!

There is no right or wrong way to play, so you will need to spend some time experimenting with the instrument, trying to find how many different ways you can make a sound come out, and then working out how to integrate these sounds into a piece of music. This is the way I approached teaching myself how to play, and I continue to enjoy the journey as I work to master the instrument.

With this in mind, I would like to offer a few things for you to consider as you start the journey. First is string gauge—be sure you try several different string gauges before you settle on the one that is "right" for you. A light string, such as a 0.010" guitar string (high E) will have a profoundly different sound than a heavy string, such as a 0.054" (low E). If you don't like the sound of your instrument, try a different string gauge.

Second, experiment with different ways to make the string sound. Try plucking it with your finger or thumb, using a guitar pick (I have found that you can get a much wider dynamic range using a thick pick), or striking the string with a wooden stick, a piece of pipe, a leather strap, and anything else that comes to mind. Listen to how each of these methods changes the sound of the instrument.

One of the secrets of rhythmic playing is using both hands to develop rhythmic drive—use the left hand to stop the vibration of the string. The right hand beats out a rhythm as a timekeeper, while the left hand touches the string at different points in the rhythm to stop the notes from sounding, allowing a percussive "thump" to sound instead—this is a powerful technique.

The diddley bow is typically played as a one-string slide guitar (although Lonnie Pitchford played his guitar-like diddley bow with multiple left-hand pull-offs—again, there are no rules). Any fairly hard object will work for a slide, including glass bottles, socket wrenches, pieces of pipe, heavy bones, pocket knives, screwdrivers, etc.

It will take a while to develop your "touch"—the feel for how the slide interacts with the string. "Touch" can vary

with string gauge and the weight of the slide, so it would be useful to experiment with different slides for a given string gauge. If you are not used to finding an exact pitch with a slide, it may take some time to develop an accurate sense of pitch as well.

I found that marking the diddley bow with position marks was useful to me. The position marks provide visual cues to help get close to a note before using your ear to nail the exact position. I have outlined a method to establish these position marks on my website, *www.onestringwillie.com*. I would advise against putting a mark on every "fret"—you can find where you need to be with about five position marks per octave.

The most important piece of advice is to have fun—enjoy the journey, and remember there are no rules—if it sounds good to you, it IS good!

Best regards,
Willie.

CHAPTER 3

ELECTRIFIED STOMP BOX AND WASHBOARD

Legendary rockabilly madman Hasil Adkins would perform as a one-man band with a guitar in his hands and a bass drum at his foot. Bluesman Dr. Ross did the same, adding harmonica to the mix as well. The ability to perform with a fuller sound has been a goal of many musicians for a long time. Today, we're experiencing a renewed interest in one-man bands, with performers such as Bob Log III, Seasick Steve, Ben Prestage, and Richard Johnston leading the charge.

The electrified stomp box takes the place of a cumbersome bass drum and also gives more old-timey stomp-the-floor sound. The electric washboard, on the other hand, is just plain fun. You can plug it into effects (try a wah pedal for some serious "Shaft" boogie) and send it right to the PA system. Build these, and you'll be the center of attention at the next pickers' circle. Be sure to read the chapter on Electrifying Your Instruments (page 106).

STOMP BOX MATERIALS

- ⟶ Old soda bottle box, or any box of your choice
- ⟶ Old license plate or scrap of sheet metal
- ⟶ Wiring harness of your choice (see page 111)
- ⟶ Silicon

WASHBOARD MATERIALS

- ⟶ Washboard
- ⟶ Wiring harness of your choice (see page 111)
- ⟶ Silicon

TOOLS

- ⟶ Power drill and assorted bits, including paddle bits
- ⟶ Adjustable wrench

40

STOMP BOX

1 **Drill a hole in the top of the box.** Drill a hole in the top of the box with a 1" (25mm) bit—I used a paddle bit, but a Forstner bit sometimes works better, especially with old wood. Screw down a license plate over the hole. Later, a piezo will be attached to the plate with the wires feeding through the hole in the box.

MIKE'S TIP:
If it looks like the wood won't withstand drilling, you can thread the wires of the piezo through the box instead. If you do this, attach the piezo before screwing down the license plate and tuck the wire end through the nearest board crack into the inside of the box.

42

2 **Drill holes in the side of the box.** Decide where to locate the output jack and volume and tone knobs. This is purely a matter of personal preference. When wiring the harness for far-apart knobs, make your wires longer. Mine are close together for easy one-handed access. At any rate, you'll need to drill three holes through the side of the box. A paddle bit works well because it makes a hole in the middle to hold the elements in place, while also recessing the knobs and jack. However, you could easily use a regular bit—just make sure it is sized to fit the part.

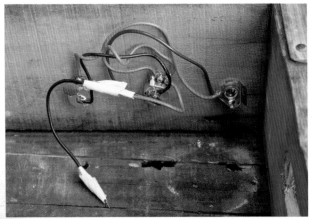

3 **Install the electronics.** Install the controls with an adjustable wrench. Use silicon to attach and completely encase the piezo—it can be located anywhere inside the box, but you can also attach it to the license plate through the hole you drilled earlier.

4 **Plug and play.** The stomp box is completed. I like to cut out small wood donuts to fit onto the volume and tone knobs to keep everything looking rustic.

Here you can see the placement of the license plate and the knobs.

GET THUMPIN'

Before you consider using a bass drum in your one-man band setup, try sitting and throwing your foot around while playing guitar. This is quite laborious! All that pedal action will make your leg tense up. The stomper is much more natural, and you can use your heel, toe, or both to play. You'll get so used to performing with it that you won't be able to play guitar without tapping your foot. To get a bigger bass drum sound from your stomp box, get rid of all treble and midrange in the PA (power amplifier) mix. Also, consider sending the signal through an EQ (equalizer) box, which emphasizes the low range, before sending it to the PA.

To play a washboard, put **THIMBLES** on your fingers.

WASHBOARD

1 **Mark and drill locations of the tone, volume, and output jack.** Once again, this is a matter of personal preference. On mine, I put the knobs on the left side of the washboard so they can be accessed when strumming with your right hand.

2 **Install the electronics.** Install the controls with an adjustable wrench and use double-sided tape to experiment with different piezo locations. The piezo must go on the metal surface of the washboard. I normally put mine on the backside of the metal, not the strumming side. When you decide on a good location, use silicon to attach and completely encase the piezo.

3 **Plug and play.** The washboard is completed.

44

PHOTO BY SARAH ANN STAUB.

TOUBAB KREWE

Toubab Krewe is an Asheville, North Carolina-based instrumental group that *Billboard Magazine* says "has essentially created the intersection of West African traditional music and American rock." NPR's *All Things Considered* notes, "Using music rather than words, these artists are showing us who we really are, and after all these years, it seems we're ready to listen." *The New York Times*: "Asheville, North Carolina may not seem like a stronghold for African-rooted music, but Toubab Krewe has soaked up the patterns and rhythms from Zimbabwe, Congo, Brazil and the Caribbean." The musicians of Toubab Krewe play several Mike Orr originals, including CBGs, basses, and washboards. For more information and touring dates, visit *www.ToubabKrewe.com*.

Dave Pransky plays an original Mike Orr three-string fretless box bass. The bass has a 34" scale. It is built with a rather large Edge cigar box. I used maple for the neck and walnut for the bridge, and an old humbucker guitar pickup.

Drew Heller plays a Mike Orr Africa slide cigar box guitar (see right). I used a Don Lino Africa cigar box with special African art, a cocobolo neck, and zebrawood for the fingerboard to really make this piece African-themed.

PHOTO BY SARAH ANN STAUB.

GUITARS

"mark top with a "X""

"mark the Bottom with a "X""

Shine

CHÂTEAU REAL

CHAPTER 4

Three-String Cigar Box Slide Guitar

The allure of the cigar box guitar is understandable—an instrument made out of a box? Can it really make good music? It sure can. Find a cigar box you like and jump right in. Before long, you'll be jamming to your own self-made music on a handmade guitar—how cool is that? Check out the drawings on page 148. If you're interested in making an electric version of the instrument, be sure to read the chapter on Electrifying Your Instruments (page 106).

HISTORY OF THE CIGAR BOX GUITAR

Blues legend Blind Willie Johnson was given a one-string cigar box guitar at the age of five. He played it with a pocketknife for a slide. Rock and Roll Hall of Famer Carl Perkins started out on a two-string cigar box guitar, using a broken bottleneck as his slide. Countless other music legends have similar stories of starting on the poor-man's guitar. Back in the early 1900s, wooden cigar boxes were plentiful and the other parts of the instrument could be built from scrap wood, bolts, screen wire, and other found objects—almost anyone could find (and afford!) the parts to make a cigar box guitar.

Today, there is a resurgence in building and playing cigar box guitars. In fact, a growing number of musicians are abandoning their mass-produced guitars, opting for a primal cigar box guitar to give them a sound deep and rich as Mississippi mud. The instruments are relatively easy to build, they sound great, and they set the player apart from anyone else on the stage.

MATERIALS

- Cigar box
- Wood for neck, maple, 1½" x ¾" x 33" (40 x 20 x 840mm)
- Wood for fretboard, walnut, 1½" x ¼" x 20" (40 x 6 x 510mm)
- Wood for bridge, ¼" x ½" x 2½" (6 x 15 x 65mm)
- Templates for three-string headstock (page 151) and headstock angle (page 149)
- Three tuning pegs, new or used
- ½" (13mm) tarp grommets, 4
- Electrical/contact pickup, Piezo element, 1500–3000Hz
- Output jack, ¼" (6mm) mono
- Round slotted brass bolt, ¼-20 x 1½" (40mm)
- Brass wood screws, #8 x ¾" (20mm), but most screws would work
- Waterproof wood glue
- Painter's tape
- Danish oil or wood finish of your choice
- Drawer pull (optional)
- Guitar strings, acoustic A, D, G, light gauge

TOOLS

- Coping saw
- Measuring tape
- Power drill and assorted bits, including ¼" (6mm) countersink and 1⁄16" (2mm) twist bit
- Hole saw or ⅝" (15mm) paddle bit to drill holes for tarp grommets
- Assorted sandpaper and sanding block, or belt sander
- Band saw, scroll saw, coping saw, or handsaw
- Miter box
- Assorted screwdrivers
- Plastic clamps, 6 to 8
- Pencil
- Square
- Rag or brush to apply wood finish
- ½" (15mm) wood file for shaping the neck
- Power router (optional)
- ¼" (6mm) rattail rasp
- Utility knife
- Awl

48

50

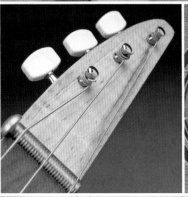

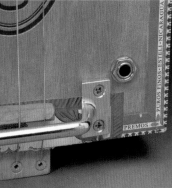

BASIC STARTING NOTES

I suggest skimming through the next three chapters to get an overview of the project and your options before building your first four-stringed guitar. You may decide you need to gather more tools or purchase a few optional decorations, sound holes, or accessories to enhance the finished instrument. Now is a good time to make those plans so you can avoid delays later when you reach those steps of construction.

FRETBOARD LENGTH. The length of the box determines fretboard length. A shorter box equals a longer fretboard and vice versa.

FINDING SUPPLIES. You can find supplies just about anywhere: think the home improvement store, electronics store, eBay, yard sales, salvage, and even the dump.

RESONATORS. Cigar boxes come in many sizes and shapes, and are made of wood from around the world. You could also use biscuit tins, cookie tins, old oil and gas cans, hub caps, and whatever else comes to mind. See Chapter 5 for detailed instructions on using a cookie tin. Flea markets, swap meets, and yard sales are great places to search for resonators. Use your imagination; you might not know what you are looking for until you see it.

THE NECK. When choosing wood for the neck, look for straight 1" x 2" (25 x 50mm) pieces of hardwood such as cherry, oak, or maple—just about any hard wood will work. Straight boards are not that critical for slide instruments because the strings are high and played with a slide, but it is important for fretted and fret-less guitars that are fretted with your fingers. Look for 1x2s at your local big box hardware store or the local lumberyard. They are usually sold by the board foot. I get most of my wood from the scrap heap at a local cabinet shop. Reclaimed wood, such as old tables, dressers, and furniture built with solid wood, could be used but would require a table saw to cut to size. Walnut, oak, and cherry will work great.

MAKING BRIDGES. I use pieces of hardwood to make all of the bridges in these projects, but another option is to use Corian countertop scraps, also available from most cabinet shops. Corian is available in many colors, and is pretty easy to shape with coarse sandpaper and a sanding block. Another very simple option is to use a ¼" x 2½" (6 x 65mm) threaded rod or eye bolt for the bridge. You may have to place a block of wood under the bolt or rod to achieve proper string height, but overall, this will save time because you do not have to deal with string spacing or cutting grooves for the strings.

f HOLES. If you are cutting custom sound holes such as f holes, you will need the pattern for these as well. There are several in the pattern section to choose from, or you could create your own.

TUNING PEGS. You can install either new or used pegs. Keep in mind that you'll need left side pegs for right-handed guitars, and right side pegs for left-handed guitars.

TARP GROMMETS. Grommets are a great way to hide tattered edges, specifically on cigar boxes, which are often covered with paper. Half-inch (13mm) grommets are available at hardware stores. Another option is to cut round holes and sand them smooth.

ELECTRONICS. Electrical/contact pickup and output jacks are available at electronics stores. Look for piezo elements for 1500–3000Hz, such as the one available from Radio Shack (piezo transducer, 273-0073). You'll also need a ¼" (6mm) output jack mono.

51

Repeat Grammy award winner **JEFF BECK'S** first guitar was a cigar box guitar.

PREPARING THE HEADSTOCK ANGLE

1 **Mark up the headstock angle.** When you have chosen a straight piece of hardwood for the neck, your first step will be to add an angle at one end of the neck. This ensures a proper amount of string tension at the nut. Place the triangular headstock pattern on the side of the head and trace the pattern (page 149).

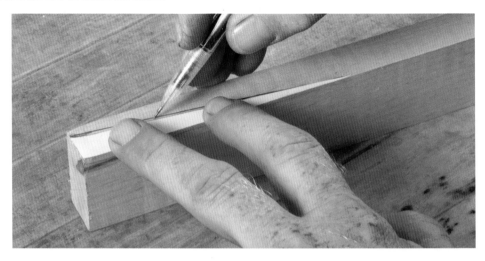

52

2 **Cut out the angle.** Cut cleanly along the pattern line with a band saw, scroll saw, or coping saw. Save the cut-off wedge; you will need it later.

3 **Sand the headstock.** Sand the headstock by hand, or use a belt sander if available.

4 **Sand the headstock wedge.** Sand the cut-off headstock wedge. Do not sand the uncut side.

5 **Mark the uncut sides.** Mark the factory-finished sides of both the headstock and the wedge that was removed.

6 **Glue the headstock together.** Apply glue to both headstock pieces on the sides with the X's. Smear the glue over the face of both pieces with your finger. Rub the two glued areas together to ensure a good glue joint. Be sure that the headstock wedge is on the opposite side of the headstock from where it was cut. Align the ends together. Use three clamps, as shown.

MIKE'S TIP:

After gluing and clamping, be sure to check that the wedge doesn't slide out of its position while drying. After about 10 minutes, remove clamps and wipe off excess glue. Replace the clamps and allow the glue to finish drying. This will make it easier to sand when the glue is dry.

★ ★

CHRIS ANDERSON

Chris Anderson has been a mainstay on the Southern Rock scene since the 1970s, playing with, touring, or writing songs in groups such as The Allman Brothers Band, Bad Company, Lynyrd Skynyrd, the Outlaws, Grinderswitch, Lucinda Williams, Blackhawk, Hank Williams Jr., Stephen Stills, Johnny Neel, Neil Carswell, and many others. His debut album, "Old Friend," has been described as a cross between Stevie Ray Vaughan, Eric Clapton, and Duane Allman. *The New York Times* described it as one of the ten best albums you've never heard. For more information, visit *www.ChrisAndersonBand.com*.

The pictured bedpan guitar was built and given to Chris by Mark Bush, who has built more than 100 cigar box guitars since getting started in 2008. As Mark describes, "I have sold most of my CBGs to guys and gals like myself that have always wanted to make music that brings them joy. Most of my guitars are in the hands of truckers who have bought my guitars at my T-shirt shop inside a truck stop out here in New Mexico. It's really cool when they come back and tell of how they have been able to relax after a hard day of driving, and that they are amazed that they are able to play the guitars." For more information, look up Ratdaddycbg on *www.youtube.com*, or visit *MojoCBG.com*.

This particular guitar was built over a two-day span. Mark notes that the enamel-free bedpan gives a much better tone than the enameled variety. The guitar has four strings, strung over a red oak neck with a bridge and nut cut from raw bone. Visit the Rat Daddy CBG YouTube site to hear Chris playing the bedpan guitar pictured here.

PHOTOGRAPH COURTESY OF MARK BUSH

53

CHARLIE BROWN, from the comic strip *Peanuts*, played cigar box guitar in a few strips in the early 1950s.

7 **Apply painter's tape.** You will need to cut notches that are centered at both ends of the cigar box to allow the neck to slide through under the box lid. To do this, cover the top and bottom of the cigar box with painter's tape.

MIKE'S TIP:
Another method would be to use the centering tool included in the patterns section. It will work with any type of box—cigar, candy, fruit, etc.

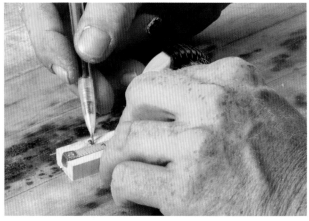

8 **Find the center of the box end.** Measure to find the center of the box and mark the center with a pencil.

9 **Find the center of the neck width.** Using a cross-section segment of the neck as a pattern, mark the center of this cross-section.

10 **Line up the pieces.** Then line up the centerlines you made on the cigar box painter's tape and the neck cross-section. Trace out the shape of the neck onto the sides of the box so that when this piece is cut out, you can run the neck directly under the box lid.

A story published in 1884, *Christmas Eve with Uncle Enos*, featured a cigar box banjo and popularized the instrument.

54

11 **Notch the box lid.** With the box lid open, cut a notch on each side of the cigar box with a utility knife or file and trim out the rough inside cut surface of these notches.

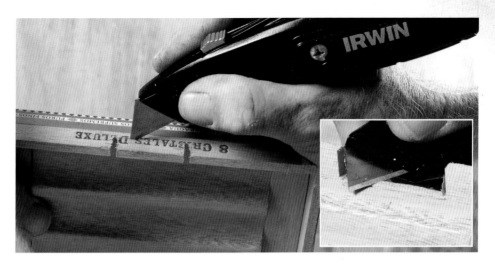

12 **Test fit.** Test fit the neck cross-section to make sure it will fit straight through the box. When inserted, the neck should fit snugly.

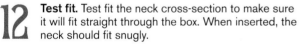

13 **Refine the opening.** Use a file or utility knife to custom fit the box so it's a perfect fit. If the hole is too large, you can fill the gaps with hot glue or wood putty. However, if the gap is small, you can leave it as-is.

14 **Confirm the fit.** Test fit the neck itself inside the cigar box to verify that the box lid fits snugly down over the neck.

FINISHING THE NECK AND HEADSTOCK

15 **Sand the headstock.** After the glue used to create the headstock angle has had a chance to dry, sand all sides of the headstock so it has a uniform thickness and your desired finish. Be sure to sand off any excess glue or burn marks.

MIKE'S TIP

Flip the pattern upside down for left-handed guitars.

56

16 **Trace the headstock pattern.** Place the 3-string headstock pattern on top of the angled down headstock and trace around it.

17 **Mark the tuning peg holes.** Use an awl to mark the three template holes on the pattern where you will drill out the holes for the three tuning pegs.

18 **Mark the string holes.** Slide the same headstock pattern down to the bottom of the neck (the "tail"). Using an awl, mark the three holes needed for the three guitar strings in the tail of the neck.

19 **Saw the headstock.** Use a coping saw to cut the shape of the headstock along the pattern lines. If desired, round the bottom edges of the neck with a router, but do not alter the portion of the neck that fits through the box.

20 **Sand the headstock.** Sand the cut edges of the headstock.

21 **Drill the tuning peg holes.** Clamp down the neck and drill out the three tuning peg holes with a hand drill. Use the size of drill bit determined by what is specified on tuning peg package. Be sure to keep the drill as vertical as possible while drilling.

22 **Drill the string holes.** Drill out the three holes in the tail of the neck where the strings will run up through, using a 1⁄16" (2mm) drill bit.

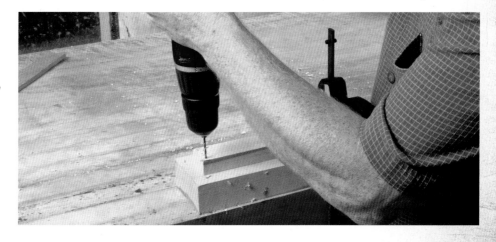

ATTACHING THE NECK TO THE BOX

Before continuing with the next step, be sure the neck is shaped and sanded to your liking. Do not sand or file the neck where it goes through the box. Make a mark an inch (25mm) from where the neck exits the box. Do not sand or file past this mark. This will guarantee that the neck fits snugly in the box.

If you are planning on cutting custom sound holes, do that next, before gluing the neck to the box. Simple round holes or holes with grommets can be cut at the end of the project. When cutting custom holes with a scroll saw, it will be easier if you remove the lid. It can be reattached later. Another option is to carve your sound holes out with an X-Acto knife, rotary tool with a cut-off wheel, or even a pocket knife.

23 **Glue the lid down.** Position the neck so there is about an inch sticking out below the box. Apply wood glue to the top of the neck where it touches the lid when closed, and glue down the lid to the top of the neck.

24 **Screw the lid down.** To further secure the cigar box lid to the neck, pre-drill pilot holes into the neck at the top and bottom of the box. Use a countersink bit to taper the hole so that the screws sit flush with the surface of the box. Screw down the lid of the box to the neck and allow the glue to dry.

MUSICAL SPOONS

You may have thought that spoons were only good for scooping ice cream and eating soup, but you can use them as a musical instrument, too. Grab a pair of metal spoons. Put the first spoon's handle between your thumb and index finger with the curved side away from your thumb. Hold the second spoon so the curved side is toward you, with the handle held securely in your palm with the other three fingers of your hand. It is important to have a bit of space between the two spoons. Now, just start hitting them against your leg, your hand, or whatever else comes to mind.

A BOTTLENECK makes a fantastic slide.

PREPARING THE FRETBOARD

25 **Cut the fretboard to length.** Take the fretboard blank and push one end against the box where the neck comes out. You want it to be flat and flush with the box edge. Mark the fretboard where it overlaps the edge of the headstock and cut it to length, making sure to cut at a 90° angle.

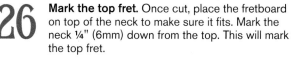

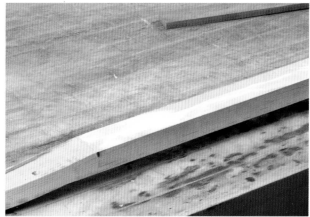

26 **Mark the top fret.** Once cut, place the fretboard on top of the neck to make sure it fits. Mark the neck ¼" (6mm) down from the top. This will mark the top fret.

27 **Glue down the fretboard.** Glue the fretboard to the top of the neck.

28 **Clamp down the fretboard.** Clamp thoroughly, as shown, and wipe off the excess glue with a damp cloth. Make sure the fretboard is squarely placed over the neck and doesn't slip or slide out of place. The more squarely the fretboard is glued to the neck, the less sanding you'll have to do.

MIKE'S TIP

Try to remove as much of the excess glue as possible, as any remaining glue will stand out when you apply the finishing oils.

HOW TO MAKE A BOTTLENECK SLIDE

1. Use a piece of masking tape to mark the bottleneck of a glass wine or beer bottle where you would like to cut it off for your slide.

2. Use a glasscutter (found at your local hardware store) to scribe a line around the bottleneck on the masking tape. Take your time and cut a solid line all the way around.

3. Place a towel or plastic strainer in the bottom of the sink to cushion the bottle.

4. Remove the tape, take the bottle to the sink, and run very hot water over the scribed line for at least two minutes.

5. Change to cold water and tap the scribed line with the balled end of the glasscutter, slowly spinning the bottle. The bottleneck will either crack right at the line or fall right off the bottle. If only a crack appears, grab the bottleneck and break it off.

6. Use 50-grit sandpaper to smooth the edges of the glass. I like to use 100-grit to smooth the edge even further. If available, a buffing wheel will give a nice, shiny finish on the cut edge. Be sure to smooth all the sharp edges so you don't cut your finger.

29 **Sand the neck.** After the neck is allowed to dry, sand the entire neck and fretboard to desired smoothness.

30 **Apply finish.** Coat the entire neck and wood parts of the cigar box with Danish oil, or polyurethane/wood finish of your choice.

ADDING THE TUNING PEGS AND STRINGS

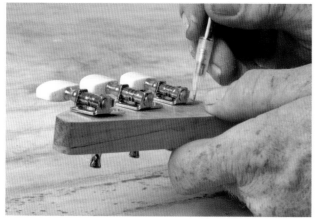

31 **Mark the screw holes.** Insert tuning pegs into the previously drilled holes in the headstock as a test fit. Remember to insert them from the back of the headstock. When they are lined up to your liking, use the screw holes in the pegs as templates to mark the pilot holes with a pencil.

32 **Drill the screw holes.** Pre-drill the tuning peg screw holes with a drill bit a size or two smaller than the screws included with your tuning pegs. Drill holes shorter than the length of the attachment screws—this way, the screws will fit tighter.

33 **Attach the tuning pegs.** Using the screws that came with the tuning pegs, secure the three pegs to the headstock.

MIKE'S TIP:

If you accidentally drill the holes too large or strip them out, glue a toothpick into the hole. Once dry, break it off, sand smooth, and re-drill with a smaller bit. Another option is to carve your own "toothpicks" from the wood used for the neck, using a utility knife.

34 **File a groove.** Using a rattail rasp or file, file a groove for the nut—I used a bolt. The groove only needs to be about ⅛" (3mm) deep. The string tension will hold the bolt in the groove.

SONGS INSIDE THE BOX is a 2008 documentary about cigar box guitars.

35 Test fit the bolt. Place the bolt. If your bolt is too long, use a vise to secure the bolt and cut it to length using a metal-cutting coping saw blade. Use sandpaper to smooth the rough edges.

36 Shape the bridge. Use a sanding block or a belt sander to shape your bridge block into a wedge. I normally use leftover walnut fretboard scraps.

MIKE'S TIP:

See headstock pattern diagram (page 151) for correct routing for strings.

Measure the scale from the top of the bolt to the exact point the string touches the bridge. There are several scales to choose from (see fretboard templates section, page 146) for instructions on making fret marks on the neck.

37 Start stringing the guitar. Feed the three strings through the appropriate three holes in tail of the guitar. When selecting strings, see the string and tuning guide.

38 Insert the strings in the tuning pegs. Attach each string to a tuning peg. Stretch the strings to the posts and wrap the strings around three times. Put the string end through the hole in the post and pull it tight. Tighten the knobs. Insert the bridge near the bottom and the nut in its groove. The strings should still be movable from side to side. Choose the positions for the two outside strings and mark on both sides of each string over the bridge. Next, center and mark the middle string in between. Remove the bridge. Using a small knife file, file the three grooves into your bridge. Be sure the marks are evenly spaced across the bridge. Replace the bridge and adjust it so it is exactly 25" (635mm) away from the nut.

62

ADDING SOUND HOLES AND ELECTRONICS

MIKE'S TIP
I suggest using brass tarp grommets on paper-covered boxes because they hide any rough-looking or tattered edges.

39 Mark the grommet placement. If you've already cut f holes, skip this step. Place four tarp grommets on top of the box. After you've chosen their locations, mark them. Now is also a good time to mark the third, fifth, seventh, ninth, and twelfth fret positions (refer to the template for placement); I use tacks or cigar bands.

63

40 Drill the grommet holes. Using the appropriate size of paddle bit, drill out the holes for the sound hole grommets. Be sure to test drill and fit your grommets in a scrap piece of wood.

41 Glue down the grommets. Apply glue to the grommets and stick them in the holes. Wipe away excess glue. Keep the box flat while the glue dries so that grommets don't slide out or move as they dry.

42 Solder the electical compenents. Refer to Chapter 8 for a simple guide to soldering. If this is your first soldering experience, I suggest using the simple piezo-to-jack harness. It is the easiest to complete because it only has two connections to solder.

The 2011 movie **RANGO**, starring Johnny Depp, features cigar box guitars in its soundtrack.

43 Mark the location of the output jack. Choose a location for the output jack. For this guitar, I mounted the jack in the lid, but you could also mount it on the side or in the bottom of the box. Mark the spot with a pencil.

64

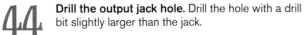

44 Drill the output jack hole. Drill the hole with a drill bit slightly larger than the jack.

45 Install the output jack. Using an adjustable wrench or the appropriately sized open-ended wrench, install the jack in the hole.

46 Affix the piezo disk. Apply a drop of silicon on the back of the neck, directly under the bridge, and push the piezo disk into the drop of glue.

47 **Encase the disk in silicon.** Apply another drop of silicon directly on the piezo disk and encase it in silicon. I have found that doing this gives the electronic sound a nice, rich tone.

MIKE'S TIP
If you choose a harness with dual piezos, they can be installed anywhere in the box or on the neck.

65

48 **Attach the drawer handle.** Place the brass drawer pull directly over the bridge and center it perfectly. Once satisfied with its location, mark and drill pilot holes and attach the handle with the included screws. This drawer slide will act as a hand rest. Brass corners could also be added. They look great and protect the corners. They are especially nice for covering the tattered edges on paper cigar boxes. When installing the handle, drill pilot holes with a bit two sizes smaller than the screws.

49 **Glue the box together.** Test the guitar with a guitar amp to be sure the pick up is working. Once tested, glue the box shut using wood glue and clamps. Wipe off the excess glue with a damp rag and let it dry. Refer to strings and tuning guide for a list of tunings that will work with these strings. I suggest using a slide and tuning it to the open tuning G–D–G. Have fun!

COOKIE TIN GUITAR

This project is a great way to illustrate that the type of resonator used for an instrument really affects the sound. The metal cookie tin I used for this guitar makes a very different sound than you'd hear out of a wooden or cardboard cigar box. Give metal a chance! If you're interested in making an electric version of the instrument, be sure to read the chapter on Electrifying Your Instruments (page 106).

MATERIALS

→ Cookie tin or resonator of your choice. Note: If you choose a resonator with a lid thicker than ¼" (6mm), you will need to use a fretboard that is at least ⅛" (3mm) thicker than the exact thickness of the lid itself.

→ Wood for neck, maple, 1½" x ¾" x 34" (40 x 20 x 865mm)

→ Wood for fretboard, walnut, ¼" x 1½" x 20" (6 x 40 x 510mm)

→ Wood for headstock, walnut, 4" x 1½" x ¾" (100 x 40 x 20mm)

→ Wood for bridge, walnut, ¼" x ½" x 2½" (6 x 13 x 65mm)

→ Pattern for four-string fancy headstock, page 150

→ Pattern for headstock angle, page 149

→ Tuning pegs, 2 left and 2 right, or for a simple head stock style—4 left, or 4 right if building a lefty (and included screws)

→ Upholstery tacks, 5

→ ¼-20 x 1½" (38mm) round slotted brass bolt, or 1½" x ¼" (40 x 6mm) threaded rod (You'll need a hacksaw for the latter)

→ 2½" (64mm) wood screws

→ Waterproof wood glue

→ Danish oil or a wood finish of your choice

→ Light gauge acoustic guitar strings, D, G, B, D

→ Phillips sheet metal screws, 6

→ Tube of silicon sealant

→ Tarp grommets (optional)

TOOLS

→ Coping saw

→ Measuring tape

→ Power drill and assorted bits

→ Appropriate hole saw or ⅝" (16mm) paddle bit to drill holes for tarp grommets

→ ¼" (6mm) countersink bit

→ Assorted sandpaper and sanding block

→ Handsaw

→ Miter box

→ Assorted screwdrivers

→ Plastic clamps

→ Pencil

→ Square

→ Rag or brush to apply wood finish

→ ½" (13mm) woodworking file

→ Small knife file or ¼" (6mm) rattail rasp

→ Tin snips or rotary tool with cutting wheel

66

68

BUILDING THE HEADSTOCK

1 **Create the headstock angle by completing Steps 1 through 6 from Chapter 4 (pages 52–53).** After this is done, decide what headstock pattern you want to use on your project. The fancy headstock pattern I used has shaped pieces of wood that are laminated to the headstock to give it a classic banjo look.
A second fancy headstock style can be created by flipping one of the pieces upside-down and moving it down a few inches. This will give you more of a custom guitar look. There are also two other easy-to-build headstock patterns that are just as functional, but require less time to complete and fewer tools. These two simple headstock designs are also available in the pattern section (page 150). If you decide to build one of the two fancy headstock styles, trace and cut two fancy headstock patterns out of ¾" (20mm)-thick hardwood, and then continue with Step 2, below. If you decide to use one of the two simple headstock designs, trace the pattern you chose on the headstock and continue with Step 7, page 71.

You may need to trim down your headstock before fitting your headstock pieces. It should be a little longer than needed. Line up your headstock pieces 1½" (38mm) from the angle on the headstock.

MIKE'S TIP:
For instructions on laying out the other fancy headstock style, refer to Chapter 6. I chose that headstock for the guitar I built in that chapter.

69

2 **Mark the neck top.** Mark the top of the neck where the headstock pattern ends.

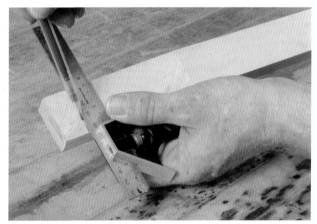

3 **Draw the cutoff line.** Using a square, draw a line across the top of the neck, as shown.

4 **Cut at the line.** Using a handsaw, miter box, or electric miter saw, cut off the top of the neck at the mark.

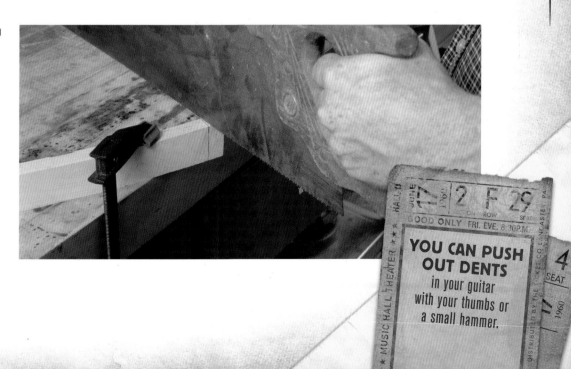

YOU CAN PUSH OUT DENTS in your guitar with your thumbs or a small hammer.

FITTING THE NECK TO THE TIN

11 **Test fit the tin.** Test fit the neck to the body of the tin.

12 **Test fit the lid.** Test fit the lid to the neck and tin body. Be sure the lid fits snugly.

PREPARING THE FRETBOARD

13 **Cut the fretboard to size.** Position the neck in place through the resonator; make sure the end of the neck comes out a few inches on the other side of the tin. Mark the neck ¼" (6mm) down from the beginning of the angle. This marks the top edge of your fretboard. Also mark ¼" (6mm) down from the end of the fretboard for the first fret. Lay the fretboard blank on the neck, keeping it butted up to the resonator, and mark where it crosses that ¼" (6mm) line. Keep in mind you'll be marking the 25" (635mm) scale in the next step. Cut the fretboard to size.

14 **Measure the scale.** Rest the fretboard on the neck; measure and adjust the 25" (635mm) scale. This is achieved by sliding the tin up and down the neck. Trim your fretboard if necessary. Remember, when you are adjusting the scale, you are also adjusting your bridge location.

72

COOKIE TIN INSTRUMENTS are lightweight and easy to take with you when you travel.

GLUING THE FRETBOARD TO THE NECK

15 **Apply glue to the fretboard.** Evenly spread glue on the back side of the fretboard.

16 **Clamp the neck.** Using an assortment of spring clamps, clamp the fretboard to the neck. Be sure that the fretboard does not shift or slip while it is clamped and drying.

17 **Sand the neck and headstock.** Sand the neck and fretboard until they are smooth to the touch. Make sure there are no glue marks. If desired, you could use a file or rasp to shape the neck to make it more comfortable to hold. Or, if you have access to an electric router, you can cut a perfect quarter-round edge on both sides of the back of the neck.

MIKE'S TIP:
To determine the correct drill bit size, drill a test hole in a piece of scrap wood, then test fit the peg to the hole. A drill press will do this job best if you have access to one.

18 **Drill the peg holes.** Clamp the neck to a stationary surface. Use the headstock pattern for the style you chose to mark holes for strings and tuning pegs. Use an appropriately sized drill bit to drill holes for the tuning pegs. Hold the drill perfectly horizontal when drilling these holes. Placing a block of wood under the neck before drilling will keep the wood from splintering around the holes when the bit exits at the bottom.

19 **Finish the neck.** Apply your chosen wood finish to the neck. Do not apply finish over any pencil or glue marks as this would make them stand out.

FINISHING THE JOB

If you want to add electronics, choose the wiring (knobs and jack) and sound hole locations before securing the tin to the neck. These choices are totally up to you. Next, mark and drill the appropriate holes. Use glue to install your sound holes by inserting the tarp grommets into the holes. Refer to Chapter 8 for simple soldering instructions.

20 **Mark the neck's screw holes.** Insert the neck into the tin in the desired position and mark a hole in the top and bottom tabs that were left on the body. These will be used to attach the cookie tin to the neck. Make sure to also trace the tab's outline onto the neck so you can mark the hole on the neck, too.

21 **Pre-drill the neck.** Pre-drill the holes for the screws in the neck, making sure to use a slightly smaller bit than is needed for the screws. If you wish to add sound holes and tarp grommets, do so now.

22 **Drill the holes and add screws.** Drill holes in the tabs to attach the cookie tin. Use screws to fasten the tabs down. Add your electronics now, if desired.

23 **Drill the string holes.** Use the pattern provided (page 150) to mark and drill out the four string holes at the bottom of the neck.

24 **Attach the tuning pegs.** Use an adjustable wrench and the included hardware to attach your tuning pegs.

25 **Secure the lid.** Pre-drill a pilot hole on the left and right sides of the lid, using a bit two sizes smaller than the screws you are using. Insert sheet metal screws. This will make sure the lid stays securely fastened to the bottom of the tin. Now add two more screws, evenly spaced, on both sides—six total. If the guitar buzzes, take the lid off and apply silicon around the lid.

26 **Pre-drill the peg screwholes.** When you are satisfied with your tuning peg placement, pre-drill the pilot holes in order to secure the pegs to the neck.

27 **Attach the pegs.** Secure the tuning pegs using the provided hardware.

76

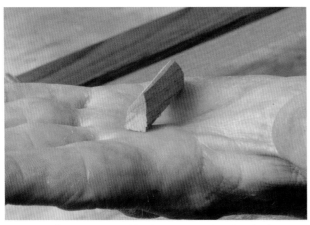

28 **Shape the bridge.** Using a sanding block, shape the bridge as shown.

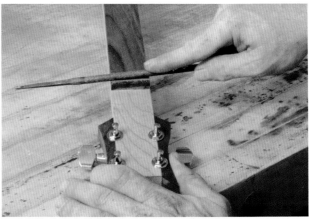

29 **File a groove.** Use a rasp to make a groove for the nut at the top of the fretboard.

30 **String the canjo.** Feed the four strings through the holes in the tail of the guitar and attach each string to a tuning peg. Stretch the strings to the tuning peg post and wrap around it three times. Put the end of the string through the hole in the post and pull it tight. Turn the knob to tighten it. When the strings are a little tighter, insert the bridge and nut. Choose the outside string positions and make a mark on both sides of the outside strings. Evenly space the two center strings between the outside strings. When you are happy with the spacing, mark the two middle strings as well.

MIKE'S TIP:
See the fretboard templates section for instructions on making fret marks on the neck.

31 **File the string grooves.** Remove the bridge and using a knife file, evenly file the four grooves into your bridge. Be sure that the marks are evenly spaced across the bridge. Adjust the bridge so it and the nut are exactly 25" (635mm) apart.

32 **Tune and play.** Adjust the scale to 25" (635mm) exactly by sliding the bridge up and down the tin. Measure the scale from the top of the bolt to the exact point where the string touches the bridge. Tune the guitar and play. I suggest starting with the open tuning D–G–B–D and a slide.

CHAPTER 6

FRETTED FOUR-STRING TENOR GUITAR

Instruments with playable frets occupy the upper echelon of "primal lutherie." While the process of normal fretting is fairly easy (as the following plans show), many builders have come up with homemade ways as well. Uncommon fret materials include large roofing staples, toothpicks glued onto the neck, nylon string tied around the neck at fret locations, and even bicycle spokes. If you're interested in making an electric version of the instrument, be sure to read the chapter on Electrifying Your Instruments (page 106).

MATERIALS

→ Wine box with a thin lid or cigar box

→ Piece of maple for the neck, 1½" x 7½" x ¾" (40 x 190 x 20mm)

→ Piece of walnut for the fretboard, ¼" x 1½" x 20" (5 x 40 x 510mm)—or a pre-slotted purchased fretboard. Note: The fretboard should be ¼" (5mm) thicker than the box lid.

→ Two pieces of walnut for the headstock pieces, 4" x 1½" x ¾" (100 x 40 x 20mm)

→ Piece of walnut for tailpiece, ¼" x ¼" x 1½" (6 x 6 x 38mm)

→ Piece of walnut for the bridge, ¼" x ½" x 2½" (5 x 15 x 65mm)

→ Patterns for fancy #2 headstock, wedge, and fret placement template (page 150, 146)

→ Tuning pegs, 2 left and 2 right, or 4 left, depending on headstock style

→ Four tarp grommets, or a sound hole pattern (page 157)

→ Wiring harness with volume, tone, piezo, and output jack

→ Silicon

→ Bolt ¼" ¼-20 x 1.3 " course thread (or 1½" threaded rod)

→ Various screws (please itemize quantity and size—for pull, electronics, tuning pegs...)

→ Waterproof wood glue or other adhesive

→ Painter's tape

→ Danish oil or wood finish of your choice

→ Ornamental brass corners and brass drawer pull (optional)

→ Guitar strings, D–G–B–E, acoustic light gauge

→ Medium fret wire

TOOLS

→ Coping saw

→ Measuring tape

→ Power drill and assorted bits, including an appropriate hole saw or ⅝" (16mm) paddle bit to drill holes for tarp grommets, ⅛" (3mm), and ¼" (6mm) countersink

→ Assorted sandpaper and sanding blocks, or belt sander

→ Handsaw

→ Miter box

→ Screwdriver, both Phillips and flat head

→ Clamps

→ Pencil

→ Square

→ Utility knife

→ Adjustable wrench

→ Rag or brush to apply wood finish

→ ¼" (6mm) rattail rasp, to shape the neck

→ ½" (13mm) file (or, optional, a power router with a ¾" (19mm) quarter-round bit)

→ Small knife file, for cutting string grooves

→ Fretsaw, .023" (.58mm) thickness (or to match fret wire)

→ Wire cutters

→ Small hammer with hard plastic head

→ Small miter box (directions for building one are included on page 85)

80

BUILDING THE NECK

1 **Create the headstock angle at one end of the neck by completing Steps 1 through 6 from Chapter 4 (pages 52–53).** At this point, you should decide what headstock pattern you want to use on your project. I chose to laminate fancy wood pieces to the headstock to give it more of a custom guitar look (Fancy #2 style, page 150). There are other headstock designs on pages 150–152, including two easy-to-build patterns that require less time and fewer tools to complete.

If you decide to build one of the two fancy headstock styles, trace and cut out two of the headstock patterns from ¾" (19mm)-thick hardwood of your choice, and then continue with Step 2, below.

If you decide to use one of the simple headstock designs, trace the pattern onto the headstock area and continue with Step 7, next page.

MIKE'S TIP:
Be sure to hold the drill perfectly horizontal when using a hand drill to drill these holes. To determine the correct drill bit size, drill a test hole in a piece of scrap wood, and then test fit the peg to the hole. A drill press will do this job best if you have access to one.

2 **Drill holes for the tuning pegs.** Use your headstock pattern to mark the peg holes and drill them using appropriately sized drill bits. Placing a block of wood under the neck before drilling the holes will keep the wood from splintering around the holes when the bit exits at the bottom of the neck.

3 **Drill holes for the screws.** After the peg holes are drilled, place the tuning pegs in the holes. Mark the pilot holes for the screws that attach the pegs to the back of the neck. Use a drill bit slightly smaller than the screws.

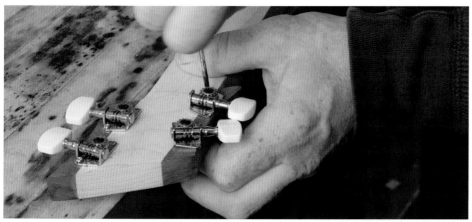

MIKE'S TIP:
If you accidentally drill the holes too large or strip them out, glue a toothpick into the hole. When it's dry, break it off, sand it smooth, and re-drill with a smaller bit. Another option is to carve your own "toothpicks" using a utility knife and the same type of wood as the neck.

4 **Attach the tuning pegs.** Use the included screws to attach each tuning peg. Test your tuning pegs; turn each peg a few times to make sure it turns freely.

PREPARING THE BOX

5 **Cut notches in the box.** Use the centering tool (page 156) to mark the notches in the center of each end of the wine box. Next, use a utility knife to cut out the pieces of wood. Another method of marking notches in a box was covered in Chapter 4, Steps 7–11 (pages 54–55).

6 **Test fit the box to the neck.** Place the neck in the notches and make sure there is a snug fit. Enlarge the holes, if necessary, by using a file or utility knife. If the holes are too large, you can fill the gaps with hot glue or wood putty.

MIKE'S TIP:

If you would like to alter the number of frets, adjust the bridge position to leave more or less of the neck above the top of the box. This will vary depending on the size of box or tin you are using. If you are using a smaller box, be sure to make the fretboard a few inches longer—this will leave a few inches of the fretboard with no frets.

7 **Locate the bridge position.** Mark the nut position on the neck, ½" (13mm) below the neck angle. Slide the box so the bridge position will be exactly 25" (635mm) from the nut. There are multiple spots that satisfy the 25" requirement; by changing the bridge location, you are also changing the amount of neck that sticks out the top of the box. When you are satisfied with your bridge location, make a mark where the neck comes out of the box.

SHAPING THE NECK AND SOUND HOLES

Before continuing, be sure the neck is shaped and sanded to your liking—but first, make a mark 1" (25mm) from where the neck exits the box. Do not sand or file the neck beyond this mark; this will ensure the neck fits snugly into the box. If you own or have access to a power router with a quarter-round bit, it is a fast and easy way to contour the back of the neck.

Also, if you are planning on cutting custom sound holes, do that now. Use your pattern and a scroll saw, a rotary tool with a cutting bit, or even a utility knife. When cutting custom holes remove the lid—it can be easily reattached later. I do not recommend cutting custom holes on paper-covered boxes. They usually end up with ugly edges.

8 **Glue the lid to the neck.** Apply wood glue to the top of the neck where the lid closes; clamp the parts together. Pre-drill pilot holes into the neck and screw down the lid. In this project, I use small brass wood screws (#6 - 1½" long) but any screws can be used. Allow it to dry.

PREPARING THE FRETBOARD

9 **Mark the fretboard length.** Lay the wood for the fretboard on the neck, making sure it is long enough to go from the headstock angle to the box. Mark the fretboard where it intersects the box. Check that the width is the same as the neck—if it is a little wider, use a sanding block to sand it down to the correct width.

10 **Mark the fret locations.** Line up the fretboard directly beside the 25" (635mm) scale fret template. Very carefully make a small pencil mark at the nut position and at the frets you are planning on using. I suggest using a mechanical pencil with a very fine point. Take as much time as you need to the make the marks line up perfectly. If needed, you can use clear tape to attach the template to the fretboard.

PLAYING THE JUG

The jug is traditionally played by buzzing the lips near the opening of the jug, and using the jug itself as a resonator for the notes being produced by the lips. The ceramic jug is the type most classically associated with jug playing, but you can play using a plastic milk jug, glass beer growler, or any larger bottle with an opening about the size of a quarter or half-dollar coin. Start playing by pressing your lips together and then forcing air through them—just as you would if you were playing a brass instrument. However, do not press your lips up to the jug's mouth.

The tenor guitar entered the music scene in the **EARLY 1900s.**

11 **Mark the fret lines.** Use a small square to make a fine line at each of the marks. Compare your fretboard to the template when you are finished. Make corrections if needed.

84

12 **Saw the frets.** Using a fret saw with a blade that is .023" (.58mm) thick (or the exact thickness of the fret wire you're using) and a fret jig, cut the fret slots about one-third of the way through the fretboard. These slots should be cut directly on the pencil lines. Use short even strokes. Try cutting a few slots in a scrap of wood to get the hang of it.

Kingston Trio member **NICK REYNOLDS** played a tenor guitar.

BUILDING A FRET-CUTTING JIG

This easy-to-build fret-cutting miter jig will have you cutting frets in no time.

1 **Cut four pieces of wood for the sides.** Two pieces are 13" x 2" x ¼" (330 x 50 x 6mm). Two pieces are 4" x 2" x ¼" (100 x 50 x 6mm). Cut a piece of wood for the base so it is 17" x 1½" x 1" (430 x 40 x 25mm).

2 Spread glue on the two short pieces.

3 Clamp the two short pieces to the end of the base, as shown.

4 After the glue has dried, glue and clamp the two long pieces to the other end of the base, as you did in the previous step.

5 **You've created a fret cutting miter box.** Be sure your saw slides freely between the boards and let everything dry before using.

INSTALLING THE ELECTRONICS

23 **Drill the knob holes.** Mark and drill the holes for the volume and tone controls. Sizes of these holes will vary, depending on the type of control pots (potentiometers) you are using.

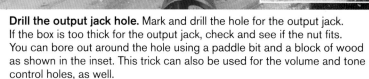

24 **Drill the output jack hole.** Mark and drill the hole for the output jack. If the box is too thick for the output jack, check and see if the nut fits. You can bore out around the hole using a paddle bit and a block of wood as shown in the inset. This trick can also be used for the volume and tone control holes, as well.

25 **Install the output jack.** Use an adjustable wrench to install the output jack.

26 **Install the piezo disk.** Use silicon sealant to attach the piezo disk to the back of the neck, right behind the bridge location. Add more sealant on top of the disk as well. Give the piezo disk a few minutes to dry before you proceed. This will keep it from slipping out of place.

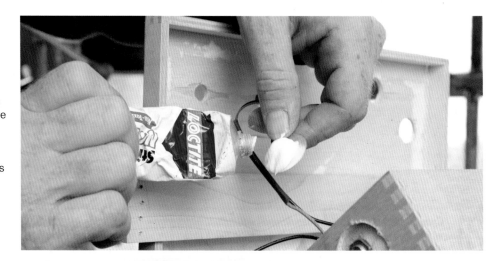

27 Install the knobs. Install the volume and tone controls using an adjustable wrench.

FOUR-STRING TUNING

Four-string cigar box guitars have a plethora of tuning possibilities available to those humble four strings. One or two twists of the tuners can take an open G tuning to a quick G minor, or even a tenor guitar style of tuning. Here's a quick primer:

1. Use A–D–G–B strings from a pack of guitar strings.

2. Start your instrument in G major tuning. Tune low to high: G–D–G–B

3. Tune the highest string down half a step and you have G minor: G–D–G–B-flat

4. Now tune that high string 2½ steps up to a D. I call this tuning "G Straight": G–D–G–D. The two highest strings are an octave above the two lowest.

5. Now, drop the two lowest strings down a whole step each so the tuning is F–C–G–D. This is the same type of tuning in "fifths" that is seen on tenor banjos, mandolins, and violins.

Please note: Experimenting with tunings can and will break guitar strings. It's all part of the exploration. Just be careful when you're cranking those tuners, and keep your face clear from the fretboard.

28 Add wood knobs. Add the knobs by pushing them on the shaft. You could buy knobs, recycle them, or make them from scrap wood. I use a hole saw bit to cut holes in scrap wood to serve as knobs. They look great with some wood finish, or with bottle caps glued onto them.

89

THE TENOR GUITAR has four strings and is tuned using fifths.

FINISHING THE GUITAR

29 **Sand and finish.** Before adding finish, sand the neck one last time. Be sure that it is as smooth as you would like. Sand off any glue or imperfections. Add wood finish to the neck and the box, if desired.

30 **Install the grommets.** Glue grommets in the sound holes using wood glue. Wipe off the excess glue.

31 **Cut and shape the tail piece.** Cut a small block of wood—¼" x ¼" x 1½" (6 x 6 x 38mm) that fits on the tail of the guitar, right between the string holes and the box. Use a sanding block to round one side of the piece of wood for the strings to ride over. This will keep the strings from cutting into the box. It will also help the guitar to stay in tune. Glue the piece in place, and use a clamp while it is drying.

32 **Cut and shape the bridge.** Cut the bridge from walnut so it is ¼" x ½" x 2½" (5 x 15 x 65mm). Shape the bridge using a sanding block.

33 **File the nut groove.** Use a straight piece of wood to check that the frets are level. Use a block with fine sandpaper on any high frets. Using a file or a ¼" (6mm) rattail rasp, file a groove ⅛" (3mm) deep on the nut line. After you file the string grooves, you can remove the nut and file the groove deeper. Only glue the bolt into the groove when you are satisified with the height.

ADDING STRINGS

34 **Install the strings.** Attach each of the four strings to the tuning pegs. Stretch each string to its tuning peg post and wrap it around three times. Put the end of the string through the hole in the post and pull it tight. Turn the knob to tighten. When the strings are tight, you can insert the bridge and nut, leaving enough tension so the strings can still be adjusted. At this point, choose the outside string positions and make a mark, on the bridge, on both sides of each of the strings. Next, space the two center strings in between the outside strings. When you are happy with the spacing, mark the middle strings as well. See the headstock diagram (page 150) for correct routing for strings.

35 **File the string grooves.** Using a knife file, evenly file the four grooves into the bridge. Be sure that the marks are evenly spaced. One at a time, file the grooves for the strings. Next, place the strings in the grooves and adjust the bridge to a 25" (635mm) scale—the bridge and nut must be 25" apart. Also, be sure to file the grooves to an even depth.

★ ★

LUTHER DICKINSON

Luther Dickinson plays guitar with both the North Mississippi Allstars and the Black Crowes. In 2007, Luther was named one of *Rolling Stone's* top 20 New Guitar Gods. His bluesy, Southern rock style has been recorded with Robert Randolph (The Word), Beck, The Replacements, Mojo Nixon, and John Hiatt. Luther plays a Lowebow CBG, and also possesses an original Mike Orr Built2Last CBG.

Luther, brother Cody, and bassist Chris Chew formed the North Mississippi Allstars in 1996. Their debut 2000 album, *Shake Hands With Shorty*, earned a Grammy nomination for Best Contemporary Blues Album. For more information, see *www.nmallstars.com*.

The Black Crowes started playing in 1984, and released their multi-platinum debut, *Shake Your Moneymaker*, in 1990. In 2007, after a few years' hiatus, The Black Crowes reassembled and invited Luther to become their guitarist. The group was inducted into the Georgia Music Hall of Fame in 2010. For more information, see *www.blackcrowes.com*.

PHOTO © ADAM MCCULLOUGH, WWW.ADAMMCCULLOUGH.COM

36 **Attach the brass corners.** Using the included hardware, attach the brass corners to the box. Drill pilot holes if the wood in your particular box is dense.

37 **Make fret reference marks.** Use a pencil to mark the third, fifth, seventh, ninth, and twelfth frets on the left side of the neck. Make the marks between the appropriate frets and the preceding fret—for example, between the second and third, the fourth and fifth, etc.

92

PHOTOGRAPHS COURTESY OF JENNIFER STADLER PHOTOGRAPHY, WWW.JSTATLERPHOTOGRAPHY.PHOTOREFLECT.COM

SUPPORT LOCAL MUSIC

When you start making instruments, local musicians can be your best friends in marketing. Mike Couch (left) and Dann Ottemiller are from one of my favorite local bands—Hexbelt. Over the years, I have made instruments for all the band members. And, in return, the band is happy to promote my work. Custom instruments like the "Shitar" (the guitar made from a vintage bedpan, shown at left) that I made for Mike are real crowd-pleasers. I've sold many instruments at local live gigs, and you can, too.

38 **Drill and insert tacks.** Use an appropriate drill bit to pre-drill pilot holes for the tacks. Use a piece of tape to mark the depth on the bit. This will ensure that the holes are not drilled too deep. I suggest drilling the holes half as deep as your tacks are long.

ADJUSTING STRING HEIGHT ON A FRETTED GUITAR

The next step is checking and adjusting the height of the un-fretted strings above the frets. At the first and twelfth fret of the first and sixth strings, measure the distance between the top of the fret and the bottom of the string. There is some room here for personal preference, but here are some general guidelines:

→ First fret, electric and acoustic: 1/64" (.4mm) at the first string and 1/32" (1mm) on the sixth string.

→ Twelfth fret, acoustic: 5/64" (1.9mm) at the first string and 7/64" (2.8mm) on the sixth string.

→ Twelfth fret, electric: 3/64" (1.2mm) at the first string and 5/64" (1.9mm) at the sixth string.

If your string height is higher or lower, you'll need to make some adjustments. The easiest place to start is with the bridge. To determine how much to raise or lower, a good rule of thumb is that it will take twice the correction at the bridge as the amount that needs to be corrected at the twelfth fret.

For example, if you want the sixth string to be 5/64" (1.9mm) and it's 7/64" (2.8mm), you'll need to lower the string by 1/16" (1.6mm) at the saddle. This can be achieved by sanding the bottom of the bridge until it is at the desired thickness.

If your strings are too low, you have two options: 1. Cut a new bridge that is high enough or 2. Build a base for your bridge that will raise it to the desired height and then glue the bridge to the base. Either of these options will work.

You can lower the nut by filing the groove it is resting in. I recommend using caution when doing this. File a little bit at a time. This can be time-consuming, but will be worth the extra trouble. When lowering the nut, use a 1/2" x 1/2" x 2" (13 x 13 x 50mm) block of wood to prop up the strings and remove the bolt. This should allow you to fit the file in and lower the groove. You will need to loosen the strings to fit in the block of wood. This will be easier to do than removing the strings.

When you are satisfied with the string height, check each string and fret for buzzing and raise the bridge to eliminate buzzing.

93

CHECKING THE INTONATION

To check the intonation, pluck each string at the twelfth fret and compare it to the natural octave harmonic at the same location. If the fretted note is higher than the harmonic, adjust the bridge toward the tailpiece of the guitar to lengthen the string. If the fretted note is lower than the harmonic, move the bridge toward the neck. Electric guitar bridges allow you to adjust each string independently, which makes it easy to get perfect intonation. With this type of bridge, you'll have to settle on a compromise that works for your particular style. Once satisfied, mark the location of the bridge with a pencil. I do not suggest gluing the bridge down, because you would have to pry it loose to adjust the intonation in the future. The string tension will hold the bridge down just fine. This guitar is ready to be tuned and played.

CHAPTER 7

IRONING BOARD LAP STEEL GUITAR

Embracing the art of 'primal lutherie' can have its consequences. When you build one instrument from junk, you start seeing other possibilities in every trashcan. The creative spark can be addicting, driving your creativity to come up with new, exciting instruments. The ironing board lap steel is a perfect example. Its flat surface and attached legs mimic the appearance of a pedal steel guitar—why not turn one into an instrument? Check out yard sales, antique stores, and online auction sites to get your own wooden ironing board. If you're interested in making an electric version of the instrument, be sure to read the chapter on Electrifying Your Instruments (page 106).

MATERIALS

→ Wooden ironing board, ½" (13mm) thick

→ Hubcap

→ Wood for fretboard, 24" x 2" x ¼" (610 x 50 x 6mm)

→ Wood for support beam, 24" x 1½" x ¾" (610 x 40 x 20mm)

→ Wood for bridge, ¼" x ½" x 3" (6 x 13 x 75mm)

→ Scrap wood, 6" x 2" x ¼" (150 x 50 x 6mm)

→ 25" or 25½" (635 x 650mm) fret template (page 144)

→ Six tuning pegs and included hardware

→ Six guitar strings

→ Black or silver permanent marker (for fret marks)

→ Volume and tone wiring harness

→ Coarse threaded bolt, ¼" 14-20 x 2" (6 x 50mm) (or 2" [50mm] coarse threaded rod)

→ Deck or drywall screws, 1½" (38mm), 4

→ Brass wood screws, ½" (13mm), 7

→ Brass wood screws, ¼" (6mm), 2

→ Brass washers, ¼" (6mm), 2

→ Waterproof wood glue

→ Silicon sealant

→ Painter's tape

→ Danish oil or wood finish of your choice

→ Drawer pull (optional)

→ Electric guitar strings, pack of 6

TOOLS

→ Jigsaw

→ Measuring tape

→ Power drill and assorted bits, including 1/16" (2mm) and countersink bits

→ Sandpaper and sanding block (Belt sander, optional)

→ Handsaw

→ Miter box

→ Knife file

→ Adjustable wrench

→ Phillips head screwdriver

→ Flat head screwdriver

→ Pencil

→ Square

→ Rasp

→ Rag or brush to apply wood finish

94

LAYING OUT THE POSITIONS

1 **Examine the ironing board.** Because different ironing boards are built differently, you will need to examine the bottom of the ironing board. Familiarize yourself with the locations of the brackets that attach the legs to the ironing board.

2 **Mark the center width.** Using a tape measure, locate and mark the center of the width of the ironing board. This is where you will center the hubcap and the fretboard.

3 **Position the fretboard.** Choose a location for the fretboard and the hubcap. Center them on the centerline you just marked, and make marks so you can replace these parts later. It's important that the tuning pegs will not be mounted above any hardware on the bottom of the ironing board.

4 **Mark the nut position.** Using a tape measure, make a mark 25" (635mm) from the center of the hubcap (the bridge position) to find the nut position on the fretboard.

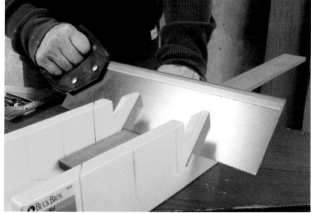

5 **Cut the fretboard to length.** Using a handsaw and miter box, cut the fretboard to length using a 45° angle at the top of the fretboard.

BUCKET DRUM

The bucket drum is a favorite instrument of many street musicians. All you need is a plastic bucket, like the one you just got drywall goop out of, and some drumsticks. Of course, you can use any sturdy stick or dowel in lieu of actual drumsticks. To play the bucket, put it upside down so the opening is on the ground. Next, sit on a crate or other low seat, and put your feet around the bucket. Experiment with hitting the top, sides, and edge of the bucket, and notice how the sound changes if you lift up one side of the bucket with your foot. Get percussive!

14 **Drill fretboard screw holes.** Using a ¹⁄₁₆" (2mm) drill bit, drill five pilot holes—one at each mark made in Step 11. Now, use a countersink bit to countersink each hole. Drive all five screws in. This should draw the fretboard tight, squeezing more glue out—use a damp cloth to wipe away any squeeze-out.

Optional: Attach a support board directly on the other side of the ironing board from the fretboard for additional strength.

15 **Reposition the hubcap.** Position the hubcap at the marks you made in Step 3; check that it is on the center line and up against the bottom of the fretboard. When satisfied with the placement of the hubcap, mark the holes. Also, drill a cluster of three 1½" (40mm) holes through the ironing board where the middle of the hubcap will be. This will be used later to install the piezo. Use a hole saw, paddle bit, or Forstner bit. Note that the hubcap is held in place by the tension of the strings and is not glued down.

16 **Drill the six string holes.** Use a ¹⁄₁₆" (2mm) drill bit to drill the six string holes.

17 **Shape the bridge.** Using a sanding block, shape the bridge so one long side has a high point down the middle that slopes away toward both edges.

PHOTO BY RJ GIBSON OF GETTYSBURG, PA.

PHOTO BY TODD V. WOLFSON OF AUSTIN, TX.

PHOTO BY TODD V. WOLFSON OF AUSTIN, TX.

PURGATORY HILL

Since his 1987 Grammy nomination for Best New Artist (Timbuk3), pat mAcdonald has continued to write, perform, and reinvent himself, releasing 7 critically acclaimed albums—5 with worldwide distribution. Some describe his style as "Gothic Americana Swamp Rock Blues." mAcdonald's latest release, *Purgatory Hill*—recorded with partner melaniejane—features an amplified Lowebow cigar box guitar, crafted by John Lowe of Memphis, Tennessee.

pat mAcdonald and melaniejane team up to create dark, hypnotic low-end grooves. The two of them onstage have an arsenal of instruments. pat has a guitar, cigar box slide guitar (aka Lowebow Purgatory Hill Harp), stompbox, and harmonica; melaniejane plays electric cello, keyboard, accordion, and a variety of hand percussion. These two carry the weight of a full band. Although comparisons as far reaching from The White Stripes, Morphine, and Black Rebel Motorcycle Club to the recent Robert Plant/Alison Krauss collaboration would not be out of line, mAcdonald's song-writing sensibilities coupled with his modification of his instruments creates a sound which appeals to music-lovers of all genres, yet has a unique stamp unto itself. The two tour regularly throughout the United States. For more information, see *www.PurgatoryHill.com*.

DEWITT COMMUNITY LIBRARY

THE STEEL GUITAR
is usually played with metal or plastic thumb and finger picks.

ADDING STRINGS

18 **Add and tighten the strings.** Feed appropriate strings through the six string holes and attach them to the tuning pegs. Stretch each string to its tuning peg post and wrap it around three times. Put the end of the string through the hole in the post and pull it tight. Turn the appropriate knob to tighten. When the strings are a little tighter, insert the bridge and nut, leaving enough tension that the strings can still be moved from side to side to adjust the strings. At this point, choose the outside string positions and make a mark on both sides of each outside strings at the bridge. Evenly space the four center strings in between the outside strings. When you are happy with the spacing, mark the four middle strings as well.

ABOUT LAP STEEL GUITARS

Lap steel guitars differ from the traditional six-string in that they are placed on the player's lap or a stool in front of the player. There aren't any frets; instead, the lap steel is played by plucking or strumming with the right hand and using a slide or bar in the left hand to change the pitch of the strings. Lap steels became popular in the 1920s and 30s in the US, and now can be heard in many music genres, from Hawaiian to country and bluegrass to jazz and rock. Notable players of the lap steel guitar include John Lennon, David Gilmore, Daniel Ho, Chuck Berry, and Jerry Garcia.

Common tunings are (from thickest string to thinnest):

→ Open G: D–G–D–G–B–D
→ Open A: E–A–E–A–C-sharp–E
→ High G: G–B–D–G–B–D

102

19 **File the string grooves.** Remove the bridge, and, using a knife file, evenly file the six grooves into your bridge. Be sure that the marks are evenly spaced across the bridge. Replace the bridge and adjust it so it is 25" (635mm) from the nut.

20 **Add string support.** Add two ¼" (6mm) wood screws in front of top two tuning pegs as shown. These will hold those strings down and keep them from buzzing. If the strings do not stay under the screw heads, add a couple of washers.

ADDING ELECTRONICS

21 **Drill holes.** Using a piece of scrap wood 6" x 2" x ¼" (150 x 50 x 6mm), make an electronics plate to mount the harness in. Decide on locations for the volume and tone controls and the output jack. Mark and drill the appropriate holes, both through the ironing board and in the plate. Use drill bits of appropriate sizes—the holes in the ironing board are just to start out a jigsaw in the next step.

22 **Glue the plate.** Use wood glue to fasten the plate over the hole. Apply clamps to keep the plate in place while drying. Install the electronics.

23 **Attach the piezo.** Use silicon sealant to attach the disk to the underside of the hubcap. Apply a generous amount of silicon on top of the piezo disk, as well. When all the glue and silicon is dry, the guitar is ready for tuning. Refer to the sidebar (page 102) for several open tunings. I like to use a double shot glass for a slide.

MAKE IT ELECTRIC

Now that you've built a gaggle of original instruments, you can learn how to make them electric! Read on to find out how to make any of the instruments in this book plug-and-playable. There's also instructions on how to make an amp out of an old tape player.

104

ELECTRIFYING YOUR INSTRUMENTS

This chapter will give you a simple explanation of soldering and guitar electronics. You can apply this information to any project in this book, and any homemade instrument that comes out of your shop. Have fun making electric versions of everything that makes a sound!

MATERIALS

→ Piezo transducer, such as Radio Shack model #273-073 or CB Gitty 27mm piezo with leads

→ ¼" (6mm) output jack mono, such as Radio Shack model #274-255

→ Potentiometer, 500K, full size or mini size

→ Tone capacitor, .033 (Check your local guitar shop. There are many capacitors available. Experiment to find a tone you like. I use capacitors designed for Fender Stratocasters.)

→ Wire, red and black, 22 gauge. (Insulated wire could also be used. If this is your first attempt, I suggest using individual wires. It will be easier to follow the diagrams.)

→ Rosin core solder, 1.5 oz

→ Wiring diagram

→ Shrink tubing or electrical tape. This is only necessary if you need to extend the wire on your piezo disk or are using dual piezos disks.

→ Piece of scrap wood (Drill appropriate holes for potentiometers and jack).

TOOLS

→ Soldering iron, 20–30 watts

→ Wire strippers

→ Power drill and bits

106

SOLDERING POINTERS

1. Always clean the head of the soldering iron tool before using it. You can clean the head with a special wet sponge available from any electronics hardware store. Cleaning the head of the soldering tool removes any flux or other unwanted materials from the head.

2. Put some solder over the tip of the iron. This is the first step to soldering, and is called tinning.

3. If you want to solder two wires together, you must first solder them separately until they are both covered with soldering at the edge of the wire. After this step, you can connect the two wires together and place the soldering head on them until the solder melts and connects them together.

4. When connecting wires to tabs on the potentiometers or the output jack, twist the wire around the appropriate tab, then touch the tip of the iron to that tab (not the wire) for about two seconds. Touch some solder to the joint. When the solder starts to melt, remove the tip and let the joint cool for a few seconds. I like to test each solder joint by giving each wire a little tug. If the solder joint comes loose, try soldering it again. If the solder joint stays connected, it is a good connection.

ELECTRONICS TERMS

CAPACITOR: An electrical device that stores electricity between two plates. In guitar electronics, this quality is used to offset any undesirable qualities in tone—by adjusting the capacitor, you are adjusting the flow of electricity that creates the digital sound.

PIEZO DISK: This device is positioned under the bridge of a guitar and changes string vibration into alternating current that can be carried to an amplifier.

POTENTIOMETER: An electrical part that allows adjustment within a range; better known as "pots." In guitar electronics, you will use a potentiometer for volume control.

SHAKER

A shaker is a very simple percussion instrument to make. All you need is some sort of container—a jar, a bottle with a lid, a plastic storage container, etc.—and some stuff to shake. Salt is a great (and cheap) shaking material; pebbles, sand, marbles, or about a cup of any small objects will work. Simply put the shaking material in the container, securely close the container, and start shaking!

108

1 Strip the wire ends. Plug in the soldering iron, then cut seven 5" (130mm) lengths of wire—three red and four black—and strip about a quarter-inch off of the ends.

DOOR BUZZERS are a great source for piezo disks.

2 **Position the electronics.** Insert the jack and potentiometers upside down in the block of wood. This will hold them in place while you are soldering the connections.

3 **Ground the volume.** Bend the tab on the right in against the potentiometer and solder it to the potentiometer as shown. This will ground the volume potentiometer.

4 **Attach the first wire.** Attach one wire coming from the capacitor to the middle tab on the potentiometer. Attach the other wire to the back of the potentiometer. Twist the wire around the tab first, then hold the tip of the iron on the tab for about two seconds. Touch some solder on the joint and remove the iron. Hold in place a few seconds while the joint cools.

109

5 **Attach the piezo disk.** Attach the piezo disk to the appropriate tabs on the volume potentiometer.

6 **Attach the wires.** Using your tone and volume wiring harness diagram, connect the wires to the appropriate tabs on the pots. I suggest twisting the wires around the appropriate tabs one connection at a time, soldering the joints as you go.

THE SPEED OF HACKWIRING

In 2007, twelve unique acts from around the US showed up in Birmingham, Alabama, to perform at a concert called The Cigar Box Guitar Extravaganza. The 15-hour concert was captured on film and became the footage for the PBS documentary, *Songs Inside the Box*. Although the cameras showed the music and instruments that make up the modern cigar box guitar revolution, there was an even more interesting scene back at the hotel the night before the show: a performer had shown up with his hackwired instruments and realized that his pickup had died from getting knocked around during the drive. But fortunately, he was surrounded by an army of homemade musical instrument builders who had toolkits full of wires, soldering irons, and even an improvised pickup winder. The cigar box guitar ended up sounding better than when it was first built!

7 Solder it all together. When you have soldered all wires to the appropriate tabs, it should look like this. After double-checking the diagram with your harness, plug the harness in to a guitar amplifier to test it. Tap lightly on the disk to test it. You should hear the tapping through the guitar amplifier. Also check the volume and tone controls. If everything works, it is ready to be installed in your instrument.

110

PHOTO BY SILVER POP POP

HYMN FOR HER

Lucy Tight and Wayne Waxing are Hymn For Her, a band that hails from anywhere they can park their trailer. H4H lives, tours, and records in their 16-foot, 1961 Bambi Airstream (comes with dog and baby). Their new release, *Lucy & Wayne and THE AMAIRICAN STREAM*, was entirely recorded in their classic trailer on a coast-to-coast US tour. Lucy plays a three-string cigar box guitar that was given to her as a gift from John Lowe, maker of Lowebow cigar box guitars. John gave her the CBG after a visit to his home that resulted in a chainsaw accident with an old bandmate. Usually, chainsaw accidents don't have happy endings—but in this case, the bandmate was OK, and the CBG launched Lucy and Wayne in a new musical direction. In addition to the CBG, the duo plays a banjo, glockenspiel, bass drum, hi-hat, and harp. Their music has been described as an "unforgettable sonic wall of banjo-thrash-country-rock-acid-blues of the sort that you could imagine Jack White having on his iPod" (UK's *R2* (Rock 'n' Reel) *Magazine*). For more information, visit *hymnforher.com*.

THE THEREMIN is often cited as the first electronic instrument.

PIEZO, TONE, VOLUME, AND JACK

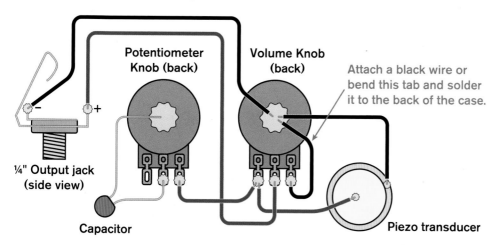

¼" Output jack
(side view)

Potentiometer
Knob (back)

Volume Knob
(back)

Attach a black wire or
bend this tab and solder
it to the back of the case.

Capacitor

Piezo transducer

WIRING TWO PIEZOS TO JACK

SERIES

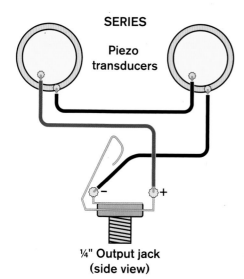

Piezo
transducers

¼" Output jack
(side view)

PARALLEL

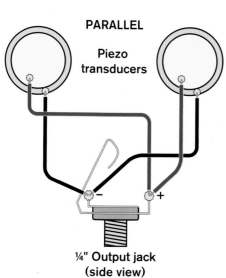

Piezo
transducers

¼" Output jack
(side view)

PIEZO, VOLUME, AND JACK

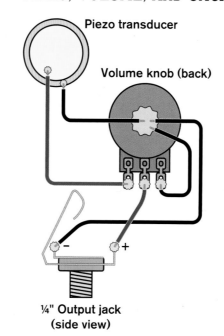

Piezo transducer

Volume knob (back)

¼" Output jack
(side view)

WIRING A PIEZO TO A JACK

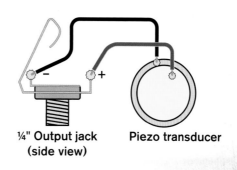

¼" Output jack
(side view)

Piezo transducer

CHAPTER 9

UPCYCLED TAPE DECK AMP

There's no reason to go out and purchase an amplifier—you can make one yourself, using any cassette player. These days, cassette players are reasonably affordable, due to the falling popularity of tapes. The radio I used in this project is a solid-state reproduction of a vintage tube radio. Tens of thousands of these were produced and sold in the 80s and 90s, under the name brands Thomas and Crosley. They can be found for cheap at yard sales, swap meets, or eBay. Old jam boxes and portable stereos can also be used. In short, any cassette deck can be used as an input for your homemade instrument, without any cutting or soldering. Use a cassette to CD ⅛" to ¼" (3 to 6mm) adapter, plug in your instrument, and play it. However, if you would like a more permanent conversion with an actual ¼" (6mm) input jack, just follow the steps here.

This amp will work a lot better with instruments that have volume controls, though it is easy enough to add a volume control to the amp itself. This will allow you to play any guitar without volume controls (it just has to have a piezo and an output jack) through the amp. This will also act as an overdrive effect when the knob is turned all the way up. Guitars played without a volume control will work, but seem to only have an overdrive effect.

MATERIALS

→ Radio or portable stereo with cassette deck

→ ¼" (6mm) mono output jack

→ Volume pot (only necessary for using guitars without volume controls)

→ Flux-core solder

→ Shrink tubing

TOOLS

→ Phillips head screwdriver

→ Flat head screwdriver

→ Soldering iron

→ Wire cutters

→ Wire strippers

→ Power drill and assorted bits

114

HACK THE CASSETTE PLAYER

1 **Expose the electronics in the player.** For this type of radio, you should remove the back. Depending what sort of player you're hacking, the way to expose the electronics will vary. Most radios will come apart with a Phillips head screwdriver. Remember to always unplug the radio before you begin to take it apart.

2 **Locate the cassette deck head.** Find the head on the cassette deck. It is usually a silver square with wires going to it. The actual tape rides across this and is read here.

3 **Cut the wire.** Use wire cutters to cut the wire going to the cassette deck head. You'll be taking the wire that used to hook up the cassette to the speaker and hacking it so that the wire now hooks up the jack to the speaker. Cut the wire as close to the cassette as possible to give yourself the most room.

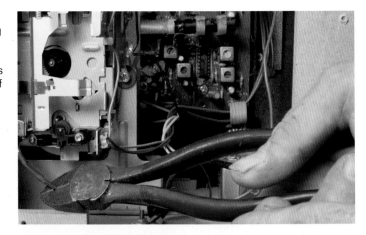

4 **Strip and solder the wire.** Strip the wire you just cut. If the device you're using has only one speaker, there will be only two wires—a copper one (the ground) and one other. If the radio you are converting has two speakers, there will be three wires: left, right, and ground (again, a copper wire). Splice the left and right together before proceeding. Solder the copper ground wire to the negative post on the jack. Solder the other wire (or spliced left and right wires) to the positive post on the jack. See the soldering section on page 108 if you need a refresher.

116

AMP, TONE, VOLUME, AND JACK

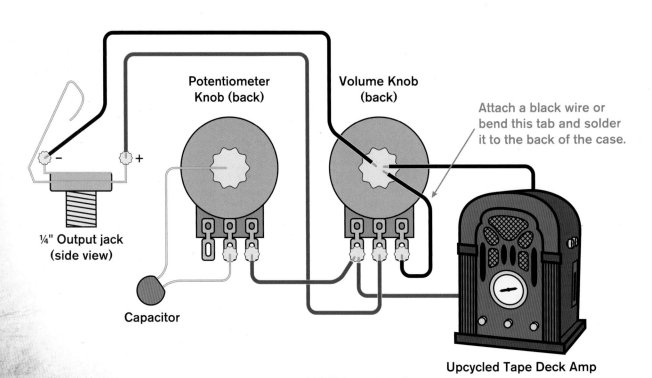

Potentiometer Knob (back)

Volume Knob (back)

Attach a black wire or bend this tab and solder it to the back of the case.

¼" Output jack (side view)

Capacitor

Upcycled Tape Deck Amp

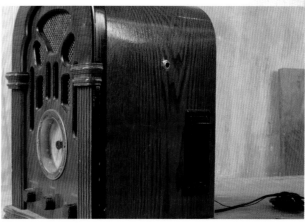

5 **Drill the input jack hole.** If needed or desired, drill a hole for the input jack and volume control. Install the input jack in the hole and replace the panel.

6 **Use the amp.** You are now ready to use this radio as an amp. Use a cassette to activate the amp feature. Simply insert the cassette and the amp is activated. Eject the cassette, and you are back in radio mode. The radio will still work.

★ ★

PHOTO BY TRICIA PERRY

HOMEMADE JAMZ BLUES BAND

"These young kids have got energy, talent and do the blues proud with their own flavor. I believe they've got a GREAT future ahead." — B.B. King

Homemade Jamz Blues Band hails from Tupelo, Mississippi, and is known as the youngest blues band in America. Siblings Ryan, Kyle, and Taya Perry (ages 18, 16, and 12 as of 2011) play guitar, bass, and drums, respectively. The Homemade Jamz Blues Band has been featured in all major media: NPR, PBS, *CBS Sunday Morning*, *NBC Today Show*, BET, internationally distributed blues magazines, and in local papers everywhere they go. The young band performs all over the US, Canada, and Europe, as well as the Caribbean Islands and on the Legendary Blues Cruise. In 2006, the Homemade Jamz Blues Band won the Third Annual MS Delta Blues Society of Indianola's Blues Challenge, and, in 2007, became the youngest band to compete in the International Blues Challenge. Out of 93 bands, HJBB took second place—their first time in a major competition. HJBB has gone on to be nominated for the "Best New Artist Debut," Blues Music Award, 2009; and to win the Jus' BMA "Band or Combo of the Year," in 2010, giving them the significant accomplishment of being the youngest blues band in history to be nominated for these, or any major blues music award.

Ryan's guitar and Kyle's bass, pictured here, were both made from mufflers and other car parts by their father, Renaud. For more information, visit *www.hmjamzbluesband.com*.

117

The audio amplifier was developed by **LEE DE FOREST** in the early 1900s.

GALLERY

Now that you've had a chance to see how I created a handful of instruments, you'll be able to appreciate that I wasn't exaggerating about the great variety of outcomes that are possible. Browse through this gallery to see even more possibilities—keep in mind that this is just a selection of the instruments I've made over the years. I hope you're inspired by viewing the countless ways the basic processes I've illustrated here can be applied to making real handmade instruments. You really can make an instrument out of just about anything!

118

SET 1
License Plate Guitar, Crappercaster,
Shitar No. 2, and Bang Bang Banjo

LICENSE PLATE GUITAR

License plates make an eye-catching and unique guitar front. The easiest way to construct a guitar around a license plate is to first build a wooden box a little bit smaller than the plate. Then, bend the edges of the plate over the edges of the box and screw it in place. Brass corners are a great touch on this type of guitar because they hide the less-than-perfect things that can happen when folding metal on a corner. It can be tricky placing the bridge on a license plate guitar—where you want to put it might be right over a bumpy letter or number. Remember to figure out your bridge and nut placement before you saw off the neck.

120

The Cigar Box Guitar Museum is located in New Alexandria, Pennsylvania.

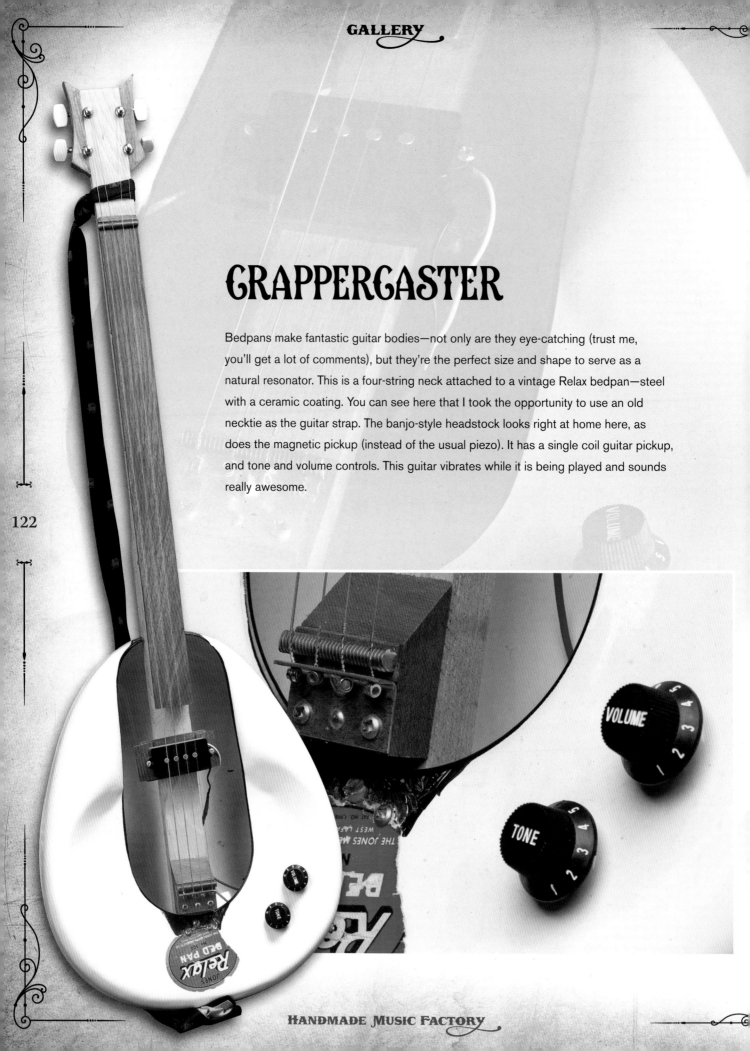

CRAPPERCASTER

Bedpans make fantastic guitar bodies—not only are they eye-catching (trust me, you'll get a lot of comments), but they're the perfect size and shape to serve as a natural resonator. This is a four-string neck attached to a vintage Relax bedpan—steel with a ceramic coating. You can see here that I took the opportunity to use an old necktie as the guitar strap. The banjo-style headstock looks right at home here, as does the magnetic pickup (instead of the usual piezo). It has a single coil guitar pickup, and tone and volume controls. This guitar vibrates while it is being played and sounds really awesome.

122

SHITAR NO. 2

Here's a second take on the bedpan shtick. It just goes to show you that there are many different sizes and shapes of bedpans available! Poke around at yard sales, thrift stores, and antique shops—you never know what you'll find.

BANG BANG BANJO

This banjo moonlights as a hand drum. Playing it takes one-man-banding to a whole new level—you can smack the drum head as you play the strings for extra dimension. This also has the visual effect of a traditional banjo.

124

THE CIGAR BOX
did not exist until
about 1840.

SET 2

Black Tabak Bass, Hubcap Banjo,
and Brick House Uke

HUBCAP BANJO

People love these hubcap banjos. It's a fantastic way to commemorate a favorite car—or to have a piece of the car you'll never be able to afford whole! This is one of my favorite instruments—if you couldn't tell, I am a fan of Volkswagons. Here you can see another way of providing a strap—braided hemp cord.

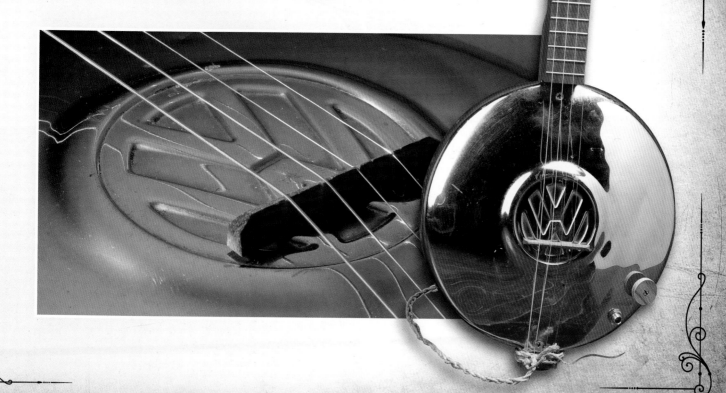

BLACK TABAK BASS

This gorgeous cigar box made the perfect start for a distinctive CBG. The pattern around the edges, the large gold logo, and the intact guarantee sticker all create colorful focal points. I put this four-string together pretty similarly to the project on page 48. The main differences are that I used beer bottle caps on top of the knobs and utilized larger rings instead of grommets for the sound holes.

128

A young
JIMI HENDRIX
made his own cigar
box guitar.

130

BRICK HOUSE UKE

Some cigar boxes come with a hinged lid, which is great for making a CBG with accessible electronics inside. Again, notice how much having a cool cigar box to start with can really make the instrument stand out visually. I used nylon strings to give the instrument a proper ukulele sound.

SET 3
Allados CBG, Spoonsby Slider, and Wooden Box Pobro

ALLADOS CBG

This three-stringer came together pretty well. I used four symmetrically placed sound holes, finished off with grommets. The simple headstock is complimented by the use of a colorful patterned necktie as a guitar strap. You can also see that I used cigar bands up the neck as fret markers—a pretty cool way to keep the cigar theme going.

132

WOODEN BOX POBRO

This four-stringer features two unconventionally shaped sound holes, magnetic pickup, and four smooth pearlescent tuning knobs. The strainer under the bridge lends a bit of a metallic sound to the guitar.

SPOONSBY SLIDER

This CBG was built for the guitarist of Hexbelt (see page 92). This was my first guitar using old electric guitar pickups. It also features my first attempt at a tremolo bar/bridge made from an old spoon. I heated the handle of the spoon under the bridge and wrapped it around a dowel rod to get it in the shape and position I wanted. The player of the guitar can move that handle to create a cool vibrato sound out of the strings. The neck is a 1½"x ¾" (40 x 20mm) solid piece of oak. There is an extra piece of wood glued to the back of neck where it runs through the box for extra support; this allowed cutting into the neck for a pickup. The fretboard is ¼" (6mm)-thick mahogany with cigar bands marking the fret positions. I used half of a Fender bass pickup and a piezo pickup. A three-way switch allows use of either pickup or both at once. I used D–G–B–E acoustic guitar strings, and an old spoon for the tail piece.

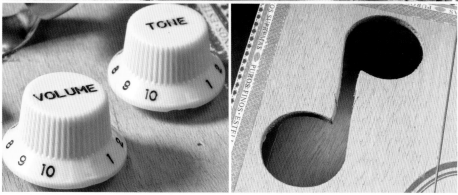

In the episode
CREATIVITY,
Fat Albert and the
Cosby Kids form a
junkyard band using
handmade instruments.

SET 4

Don Tomas CBG, Turpentine Guitar,
and D Tin Three-String

DON TOMAS CBG

This bright yellow cigar box really played well visually with the brass grommets and corners. My favorite beer bottlecap has yellow and ties in great. This fretted beauty was built really similarly to the guitar on page 78.

Ð TIN THREE~STRING

Here's another example of the resonator inspiring the build. This unique tin has a flat side, which makes the instrument really stable for sitting on edge. The cool scrollwork around the edge of the tin inspired the placement of the sound holes and other elements on the body itself. I used a 25½" (647.7mm) fret length and a dulcimer scale.

138

139

Most major music **ENCYCLOPEDIAS** do not yet have the cigar box guitar as an entry.

MUSIC HALL THEATER

HALL
JUNE 17 1960
2 F 29
SECTION ROW SEAT
GOOD ONLY · FRI. EVE. 8:30 P.M.
DISTRIBUTED BY THE TICKET CO. LANCASTER, PA.
4
SEAT
17
1960

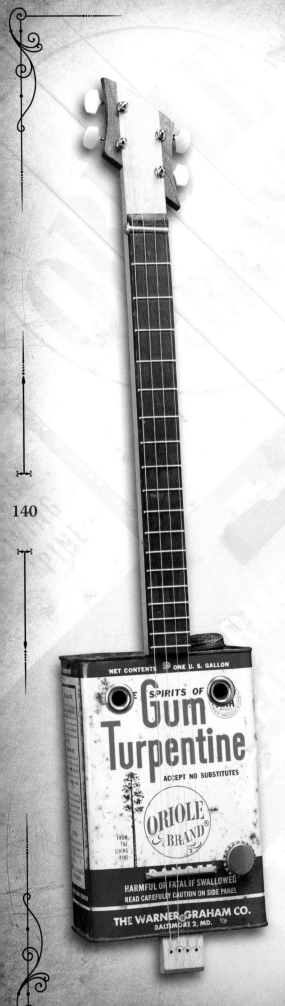

140

TURPENTINE GUITAR

Just goes to show you can make a guitar out of anything! This antique gum turpentine can got a second life as a four-string guitar. You might not think that an all-metal resonator would make a good sound, but you'd be wrong. Try it for yourself and see! I used a 23" (584.2mm) fret length and a tenor scale tuned to C—D—G—A.

NET CONTENTS ONE U. S. GALLON

SPIRITS OF
Gum
Turpentine
ACCEPT NO SUBSTITUTES

ORIOLE BRAND®

ATAL IF SWALLOWED
AUTION ON SIDE PANEL

Rumor has it that
LOUIS ARMSTRONG'S
first instrument was
a cigar box guitar.

APPENDIX

PATTERNS AND TEMPLATES

142

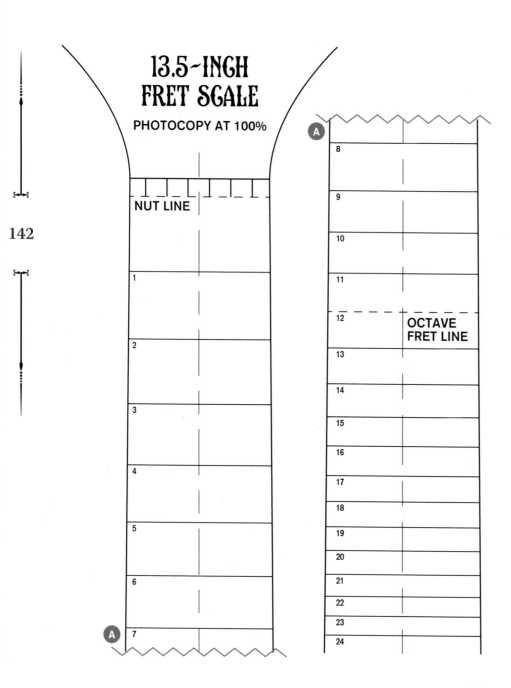

13.5-INCH
FRET SCALE

PHOTOCOPY AT 100%

NUT LINE

OCTAVE
FRET LINE

FRET SCALE
UKULELE

Fret number	Distance to fret from nut	
1	0.758"	19.245mm
2	1.473"	37.411mm
3	2.148"	54.557mm
4	2.785"	70.740mm
5	3.386"	86.015mm
6	3.954"	100.433mm
7	4.490"	114.042mm
8	4.996"	126.887mm
9	5.473"	139.010mm
10	5.923"	150.454mm
11	6.349"	161.255mm
12	6.750"	171.450mm
13	7.129"	181.073mm
14	7.486"	190.155mm
15	7.824"	198.728mm
16	8.143"	206.820mm
17	8.443"	214.458mm
18	8.727"	221.667mm
19	8.995"	228.471mm
20	9.248"	234.893mm
21	9.486"	240.955mm
22	9.712"	246.677mm
23	9.924"	252.078mm
24	10.125"	257.175mm

23-INCH
FRET SCALE

PHOTOCOPY AT 100%

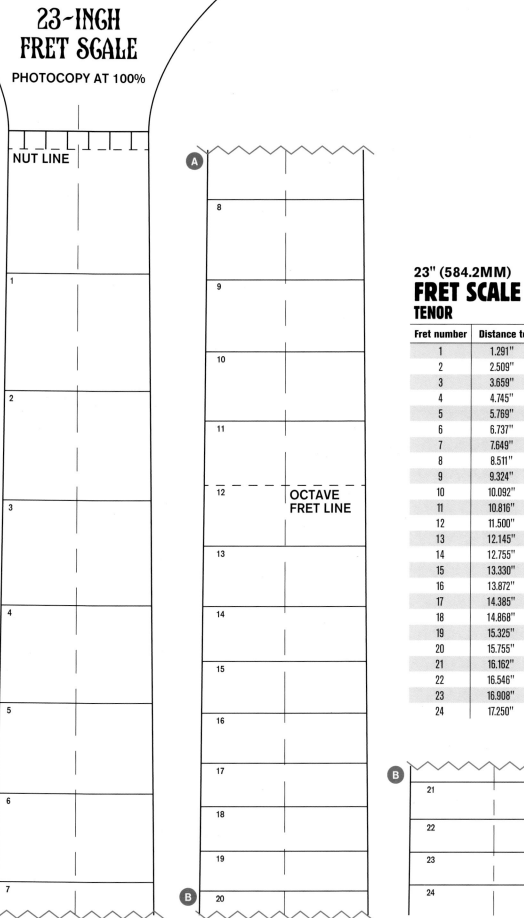

NUT LINE

A

8

9

10

11

12 OCTAVE
    FRET LINE

13

14

15

16

17

18

19

B 20

1

2

3

4

5

6

A 7

23" (584.2MM)
FRET SCALE
TENOR

Fret number	Distance to fret from nut	
1	1.291"	32.789mm
2	2.509"	63.737mm
3	3.659"	92.948mm
4	4.745"	120.520mm
5	5.769"	146.545mm
6	6.737"	171.108mm
7	7.649"	194.293mm
8	8.511"	216.177mm
9	9.324"	236.833mm
10	10.092"	256.329mm
11	10.816"	274.731mm
12	11.500"	292.100mm
13	12.145"	308.494mm
14	12.755"	323.968mm
15	13.330"	338.574mm
16	13.872"	352.360mm
17	14.385"	365.372mm
18	14.868"	377.654mm
19	15.325"	389.247mm
20	15.755"	400.189mm
21	16.162"	410.516mm
22	16.546"	420.264mm
23	16.908"	429.465mm
24	17.250"	438.150mm

143

B

21

22

23

24

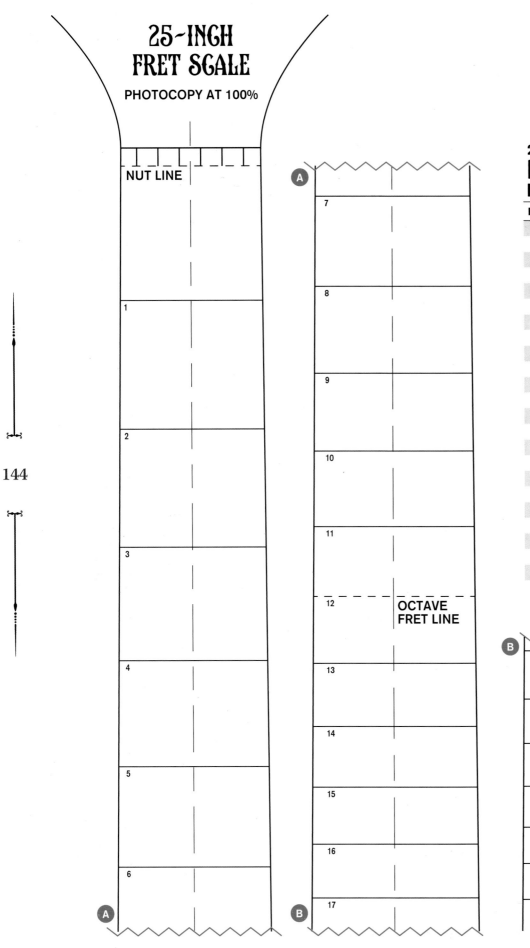

25-INCH FRET SCALE

PHOTOCOPY AT 100%

NUT LINE

1
2
3
4
5
6

A
7
8
9
10
11
12 OCTAVE FRET LINE
13
14
15
16
17
B

144

25" (635MM)
FRET SCALE
DOBRO, PRS

Fret number	Distance to fret from nut	
1	1.403"	35.640mm
2	2.728"	69.279mm
3	3.978"	101.031mm
4	5.157"	131.000mm
5	6.271"	159.288mm
6	7.322"	185.987mm
7	8.315"	211.188mm
8	9.251"	234.975mm
9	10.135"	257.427mm
10	10.969"	278.618mm
11	11.757"	298.620mm
12	12.500"	317.500mm
13	13.202"	335.320mm
14	13.864"	352.140mm
15	14.489"	368.015mm
16	15.079"	383.000mm
17	15.636"	397.144mm
18	16.161"	410.494mm
19	16.657"	423.094mm
20	17.125"	434.988mm
21	17.567"	446.213mm
22	17.985"	456.809mm
23	18.378"	466.810mm
24	18.750"	476.250mm

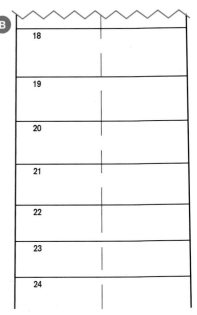

B
18
19
20
21
22
23
24

25.5-INCH
FRET SCALE

PHOTOCOPY AT 100%

NUT LINE

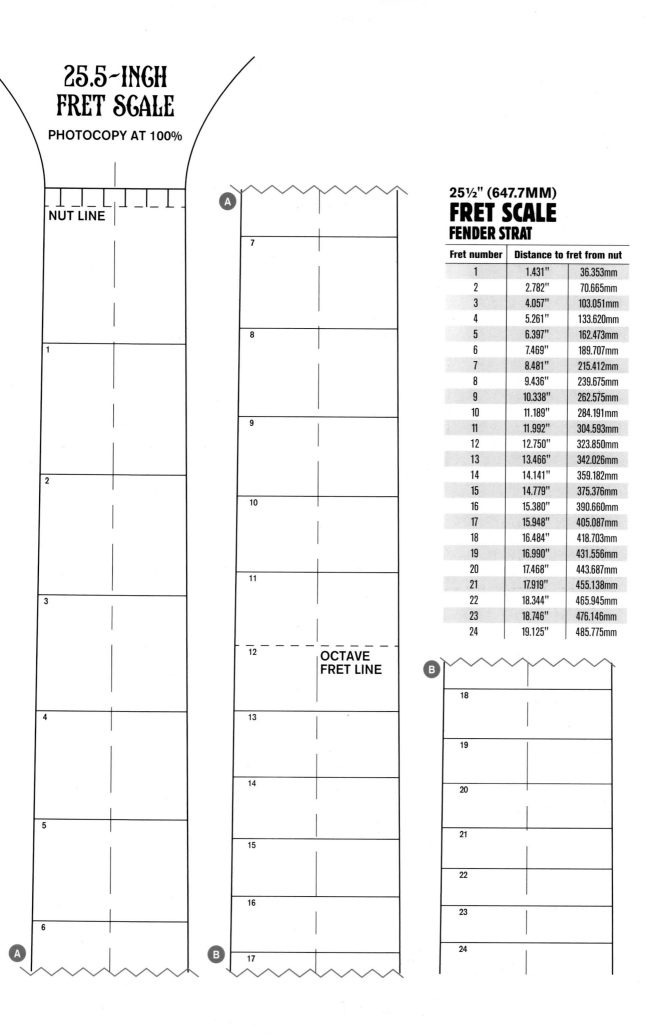

25½" (647.7MM)
FRET SCALE
FENDER STRAT

Fret number	Distance to fret from nut	
1	1.431"	36.353mm
2	2.782"	70.665mm
3	4.057"	103.051mm
4	5.261"	133.620mm
5	6.397"	162.473mm
6	7.469"	189.707mm
7	8.481"	215.412mm
8	9.436"	239.675mm
9	10.338"	262.575mm
10	11.189"	284.191mm
11	11.992"	304.593mm
12	12.750"	323.850mm
13	13.466"	342.026mm
14	14.141"	359.182mm
15	14.779"	375.376mm
16	15.380"	390.660mm
17	15.948"	405.087mm
18	16.484"	418.703mm
19	16.990"	431.556mm
20	17.468"	443.687mm
21	17.919"	455.138mm
22	18.344"	465.945mm
23	18.746"	476.146mm
24	19.125"	485.775mm

145

OCTAVE
FRET LINE

26-INCH
FRET SCALE

PHOTOCOPY AT 100%

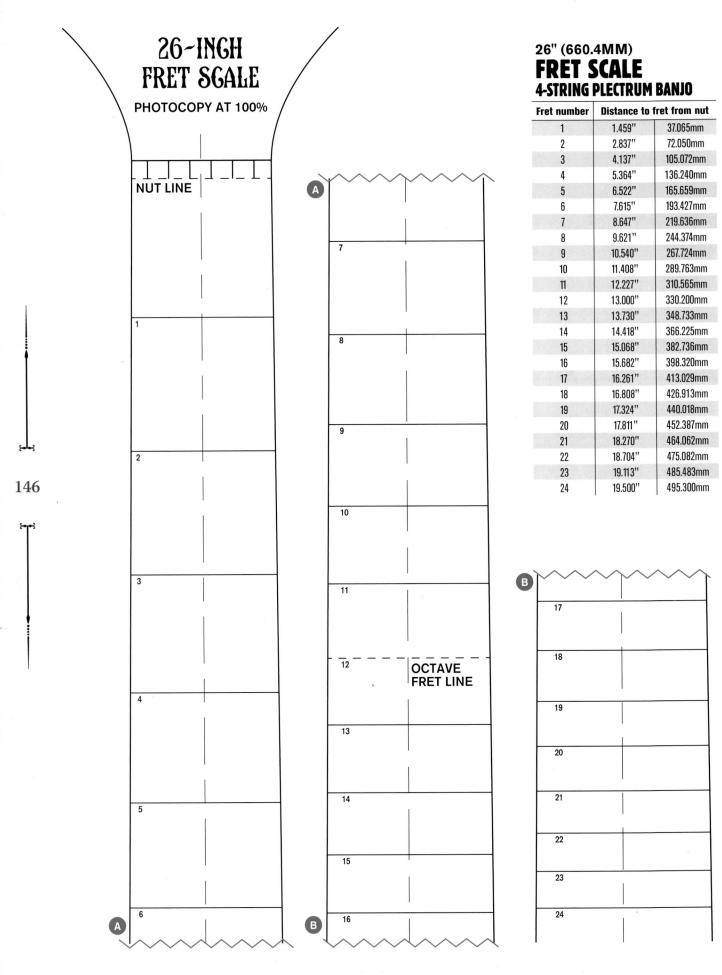

NUT LINE

OCTAVE
FRET LINE

146

26" (660.4MM)
FRET SCALE
4-STRING PLECTRUM BANJO

Fret number	Distance to fret from nut	
1	1.459"	37.065mm
2	2.837"	72.050mm
3	4.137"	105.072mm
4	5.364"	136.240mm
5	6.522"	165.659mm
6	7.615"	193.427mm
7	8.647"	219.636mm
8	9.621"	244.374mm
9	10.540"	267.724mm
10	11.408"	289.763mm
11	12.227"	310.565mm
12	13.000"	330.200mm
13	13.730"	348.733mm
14	14.418"	366.225mm
15	15.068"	382.736mm
16	15.682"	398.320mm
17	16.261"	413.029mm
18	16.808"	426.913mm
19	17.324"	440.018mm
20	17.811"	452.387mm
21	18.270"	464.062mm
22	18.704"	475.082mm
23	19.113"	485.483mm
24	19.500"	495.300mm

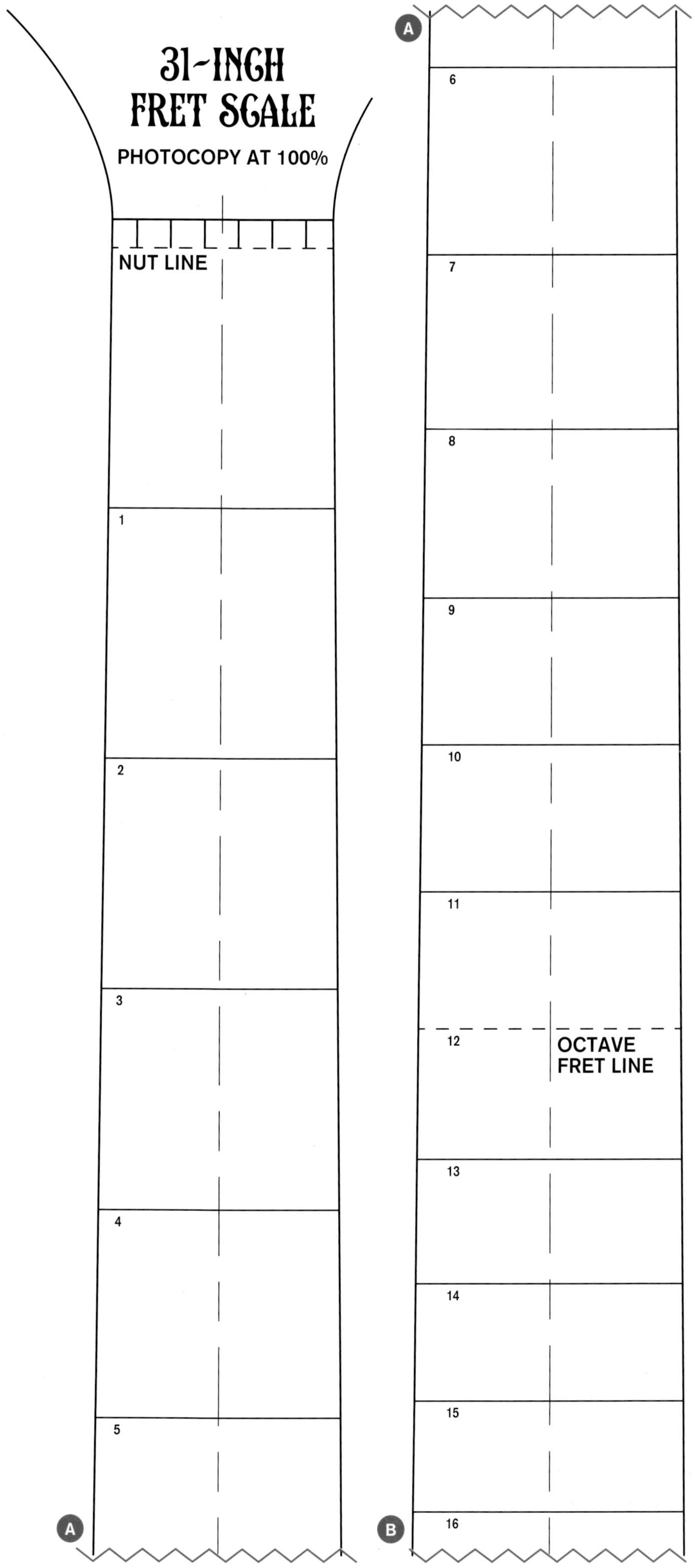

31-INCH
FRET SCALE

PHOTOCOPY AT 100%

NUT LINE

1

2

3

4

5

A

A

6

7

8

9

10

11

12 — OCTAVE FRET LINE

13

14

15

16

B

31" (787.4MM)
FRET SCALE
¾ BASS

Fret number	Distance to fret from nut	
1	1.740"	44.193mm
2	3.382"	85.906mm
3	4.932"	125.278mm
4	6.395"	162.440mm
5	7.776"	197.517mm
6	9.080"	230.624mm
7	10.310"	261.874mm
8	11.471"	291.369mm
9	12.567"	319.209mm
10	13.602"	345.487mm
11	14.578"	370.289mm
12	15.500"	393.700mm
13	16.370"	415.797mm
14	17.191"	436.653mm
15	17.966"	456.339mm
16	18.698"	474.920mm
17	19.388"	492.458mm
18	20.040"	509.012mm
19	20.655"	524.637mm
20	21.236"	539.385mm
21	21.784"	553.305mm
22	22.301"	566.443mm
23	22.789"	578.845mm
24	23.250"	590.550mm

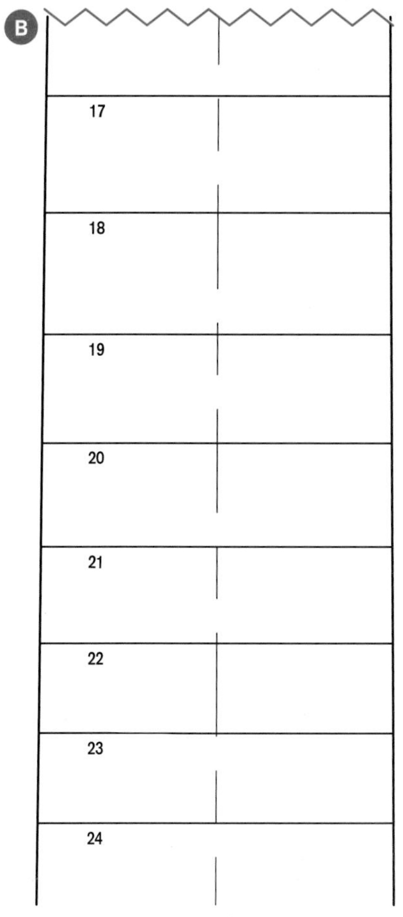

147

B

17

18

19

20

21

22

23

24

HEADSTOCK PATTERNS AND STRINGING DIAGRAMS

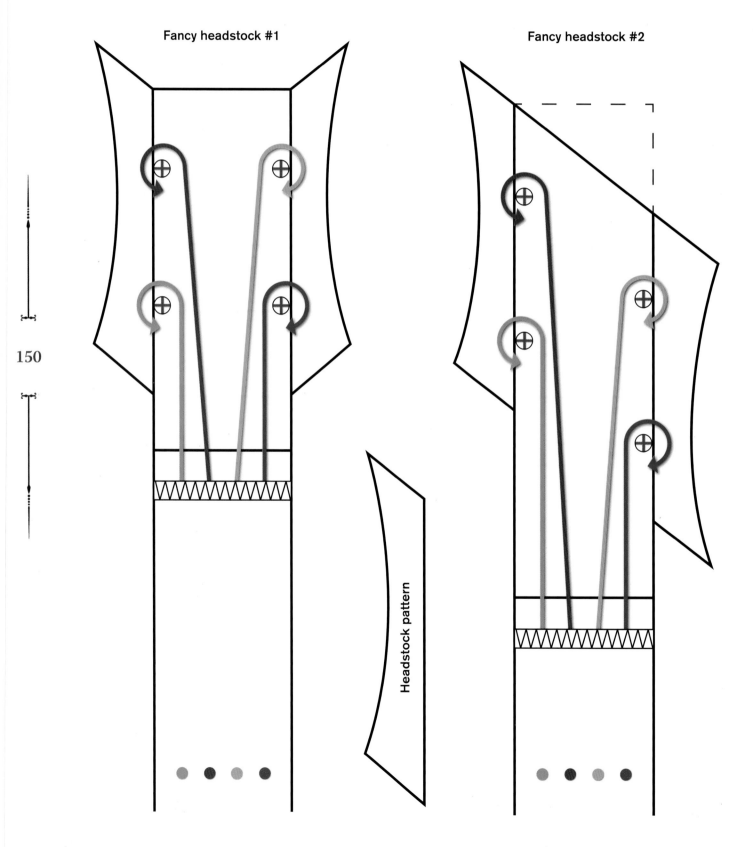

Fancy headstock #1

Fancy headstock #2

Headstock pattern

150

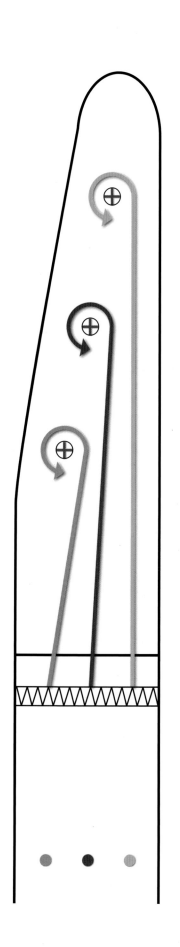

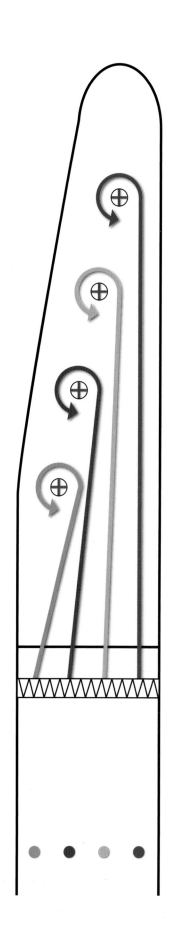

151

SPEAL CBG ORIGINAL

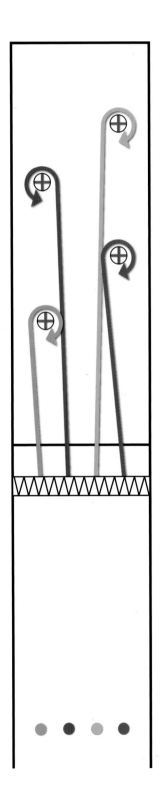

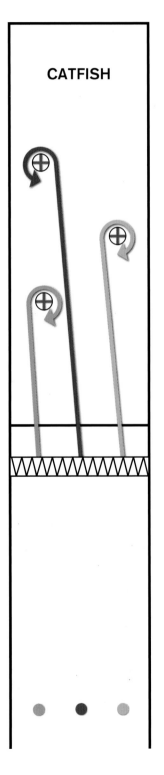

CATFISH

152

WASHTUB BASS PATTERNS

See page 20 for instructions.

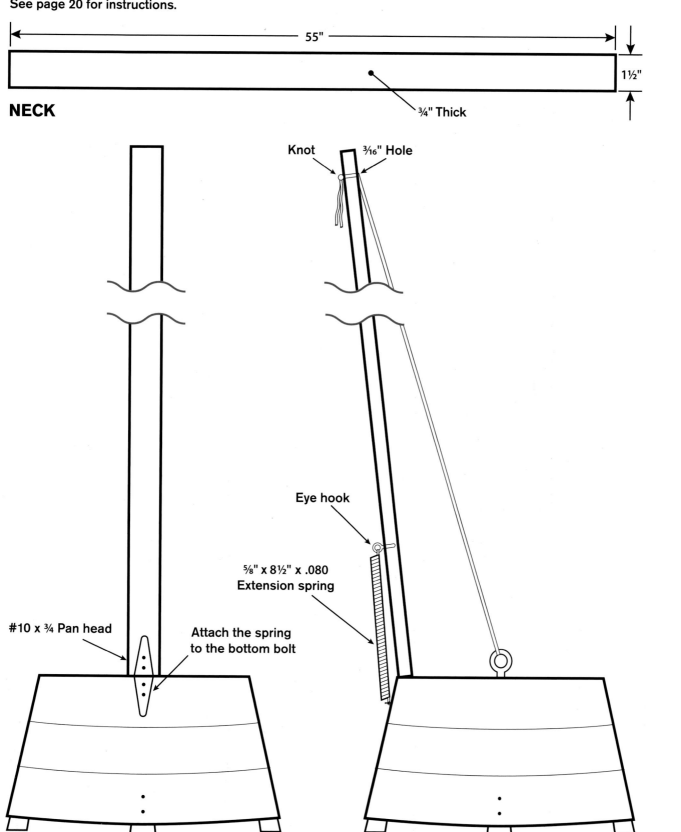

55"

1½"

NECK

¾" Thick

Knot   ³⁄₁₆" Hole

Eye hook

⅝" x 8½" x .080
Extension spring

#10 x ¾ Pan head

Attach the spring
to the bottom bolt

153

WASHTUB BASS PATTERNS

ADDING THE LEGS

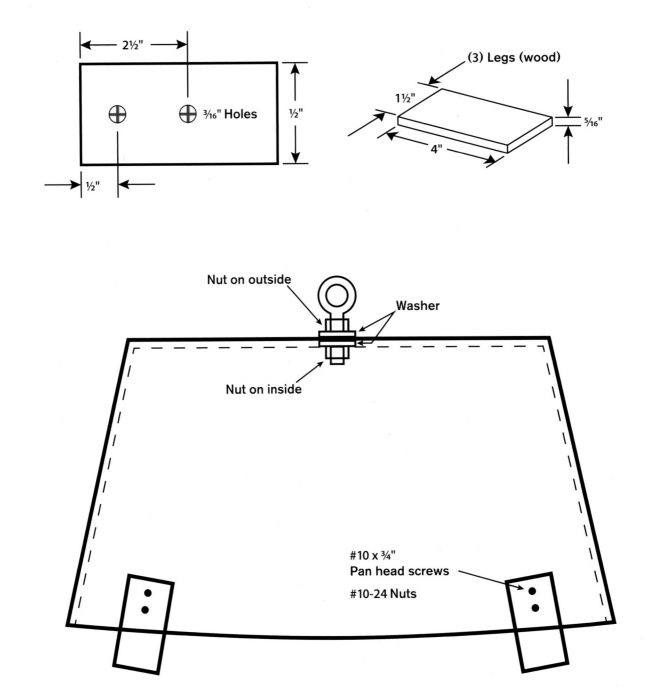

2½"

3/16" Holes

½"

½"

(3) Legs (wood)

1½"

4"

5/16"

Nut on outside

Washer

Nut on inside

#10 x ¾"
Pan head screws

#10-24 Nuts

154

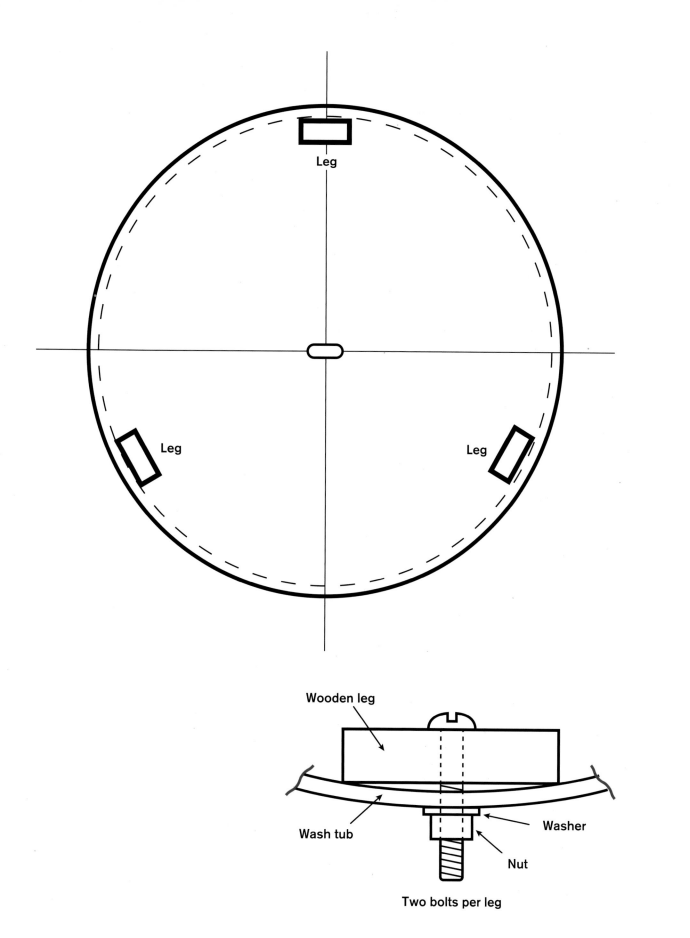

Leg

Leg

Leg

155

Wooden leg

Wash tub

Washer

Nut

Two bolts per leg

APPENDIX

CENTERING TOOL PATTERN

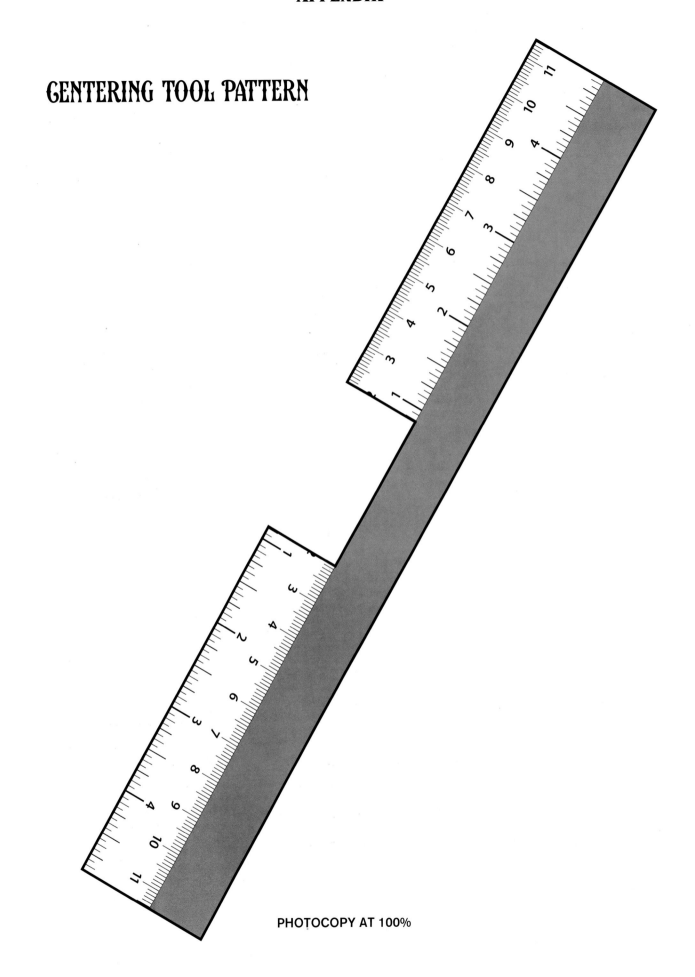

156

PHOTOCOPY AT 100%

SOUND HOLE PATTERNS

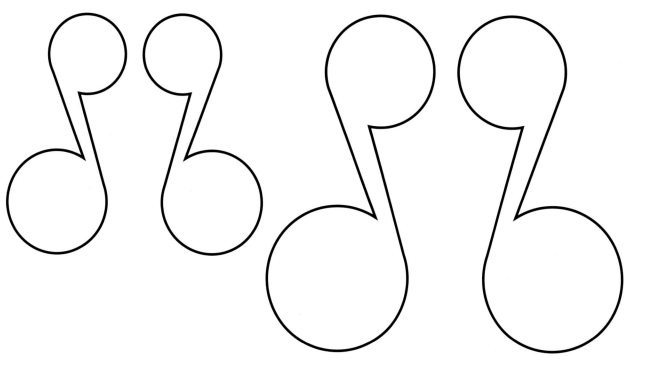

PHOTOCOPY AT 100%

ELECTRIC GUITAR PICKUP

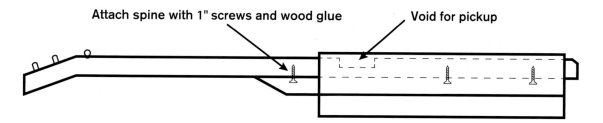

Attach spine with 1" screws and wood glue   Void for pickup

If you want to install an electric guitar pickup, you will need to create this void in the neck of the guitar. When wiring, use the simple piezo diagram and swap in the pickup for the piezo.

RESOURCES

CONTRIBUTORS

MIKE ORR . . . . *B2LHandmadeMusic.com, handmademusicfactory.com,*
www.youtube.com/cigarboxer

SHANE SPEAL
Cigar Box Nation . . . . *www.Cigarboxnation.com, CigarBoxGuitar.com*

MARK BUSH
Rat Daddy CBGs . . . . *www.youtube.com/RatDaddyCBG, MojoCBG.com*

FEATURED MUSICIANS

OTHER RESOURCES

EXPERIMENTAL MUSICAL INSTRUMENTS . . . .*windworld.com*

HANDMADE MUSIC CLUBHOUSE . . . . *handmademusic.ning.com*

HOMEMADE INSTRUMENTS A-Z . . . . *homeschooling.gomilpitas.com/explore/homemademusic.htm*

ODD MUSIC . . . . *www.oddmusic.com*

MUSICAL INSTRUMENT MAKERS FORUM . . . .*www.mimf.com*

SPEAL'S TAVERN, THE SITE OF THE NATIONAL CIGAR BOX GUITAR MUSEUM . . . .*spealstavern.com*

CB GITTY . . . . *www.CBgitty.com*

INDEX

NOTE: ENTRIES IN BOLD INDICATE PROJECTS.

ACQUISITION EDITOR: Peg Couch **ASSISTANT EDITOR:** Katie Weeber **COPY EDITORS:** Paul Hambke and Heather Stauffer **COVER & LAYOUT DESIGNER:** Jason Deller
COVER & STEP-BY-STEP PHOTOGRAPHER: Scott Kriner **DEVELOPMENTAL EDITOR:** Kerri Landis **PROOFREADER:** Debbie Henry **INDEXER:** Jay Kreider

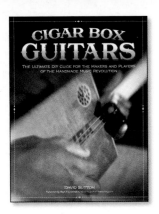

Art of the Cigar Box Guitar
The Movement of Making and Celebrating an American Treasure
By David Sutton

Part DIY guide, part scrapbook—this book takes you behind the music to get a glimpse into the faces, places, and workshops of the cigar box revolution.

ISBN: 978-1-56523-547-2
$24.95 • 144 Pages

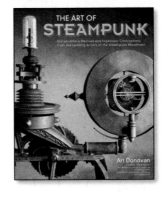

The Art of Steampunk
Extraordinary Devices and Ingenious Contraptions from the Leading Artists of the Steampunk Movement
By Art Donovan

Dive into the world of steampunk, where machines are functional pieces of art and the design is only as limited as the artist's imagination.

ISBN: 978-1-56523-573-1
$19.95 • 128 Pages

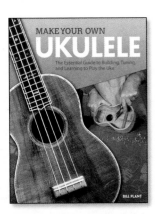

Make Your Own Ukulele
The Essential Guide to Building, Tuning, and Learning to Play the Uke
By Bill Plant

Learn how to make two different ukuleles: a beginner's basic box-shaped uke and a professional-grade soprano ukulele.

ISBN: 978-1-56523-565-6
$17.95 • 128 Pages

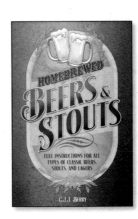

Homebrewed Beers & Stouts
Full Instructions for All Types of Classic Beers, Stouts, and Lagers
By C.J.J. Berry

Learn how to brew your own great-tasting beer at home with more than 70 recipes from a light summer ale to an authentic stout.

ISBN: 978-1-56523-601-1
$14.95 • 176 Pages

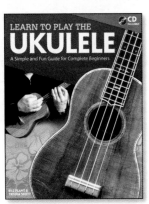

Learn to Play the Ukulele
A Simple and Fun Guide for Complete Beginners
By Bill Plant and Trishia Scott

With the help of this book and companion CD, anyone can learn to play the ukulele overnight.

ISBN: 978-1-56523-687-5
$17.95 • 64 Pages

Tree Craft
35 Rustic Projects that Bring the Outdoors In
By Chris Lubkemann

Beautify your home with rustic accents made from twigs and branches. More than 35 eco-chic projects for a coat rack, curtain rods, candle holders, desk sets, picture frames, a table, and more.

ISBN: 978-1-56523-455-0
$19.95 • 128 Pages

Art of the Chicken Coop
A Fun and Essential Guide to Housing Your Peeps
By Chris Gleason

Hop on board the backyard chicken-raising trend! Use your woodworking skills and the fun designs in this book to build your flock a stylish coop.

ISBN: 978-1-56523-542-7
$19.95 • 160 Pages

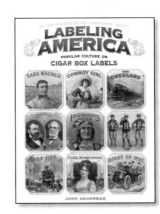

Labeling America: Popular Culture on Cigar Box Labels
The Story of George Schlegel Lithographers, 1849-1971
By John Grossman

Discover the beauty of cigar box labels and bands from the 19th and 20th centuries, printed by George Schlegel Lithographers, collected by John Grossman, and currently housed at the Winterthur Museum in Delaware.

ISBN: 978-1-56523-545-8
$39.95 • 320 Pages

Look for These Books at Your Local Bookstore

To order direct, call **800-457-9112** or visit *www.FoxChapelPublishing.com*

By mail, please send check or money order + S&H to:
Fox Chapel Publishing, 1970 Broad Street, East Petersburg, PA 17520

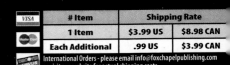

# Item	Shipping Rate	
1 Item	$3.99 US	$8.98 CAN
Each Additional	.99 US	$3.99 CAN

International Orders - please email info@foxchapelpublishing.com or visit our website for actual shipping costs.